Income Justice
in Ukraine

Income Justice
in Ukraine

A Factorial Survey Study

By

Kseniia Gatskova

Cambridge
Scholars
Publishing

Income Justice in Ukraine: A Factorial Survey Study

By Kseniia Gatskova

This book first published 2015

Cambridge Scholars Publishing

Lady Stephenson Library, Newcastle upon Tyne, NE6 2PA, UK

British Library Cataloguing in Publication Data
A catalogue record for this book is available from the British Library

ISBN (10): 1-4438-6886-8
ISBN (13): 978-1-4438-6886-0

CONTENTS

LIST OF TABLES

LIST OF FIGURES

PREFACE AND ACKNOWLEDGEMENTS

This book is based on a PhD dissertation defended on December 10, 2013 at the University of Konstanz (Head of the examination commission: Prof. Dr. Werner Georg, first referee: Prof. Dr. Thomas Hinz, second referee: Prof. Dr. Irena Kogan).

I wish to express my gratitude for the numerous suggestions, detailed comments and critical remarks of my scientific supervisor Prof. Dr. Thomas Hinz, whose patience and support helped me to finish this research work. I am also deeply grateful for the most valuable feedback from Dr. Katrin Auspurg, who taught me a great deal about quality of social research and data analysis.

For fruitful discussions on many theoretical issues and challenges of transformation in the post-Soviet countries, I would like to thank Maxim Gatskov, my husband and a social scientist, whose opinion I respect enormously and whose moral encouragement I infinitely esteem.

The empirical data analysis presented in this work is based on the survey data collected as a part of the German Research Foundation research project "The factorial survey as a method for measuring attitudes in population surveys" (Research directors: Prof. Dr. Thomas Hinz, Prof. Dr. Stefan Liebig, Researchers: Dr. Katrin Auspurg, Carsten Sauer, Cooperation Partner: Prof. Dr. Guillermina Jasso. Priority Programme 1292 on Survey Methodology; grant number HI 680/7-1). The financial support of the German Research Foundation for collecting the data in Ukraine is gratefully acknowledged.

I am thankful to the Institute of Sociology of National Academy of Sciences in Ukraine for the assistance in collecting and coding the data and for the kind support of Prof. Dr. Evgeniy Golovakha, Prof. Dr. Andrii Gorbachyk, Dr. Oleksandr Stehniy, Dr. Tetiana Lubyva, and Dr. Tetiana Nikitina.

I would also like to thank the German Academic Exchange Service (DAAD) for financial support in the academic year 2010/2011.

There are many people who contributed to the development of my professional skills and knowledge during writing of this work, among them: Dr. Anne Niedermann, Prof. Dr. Siegfried Gabler, Dr. Matthias Ganninger, Dr. Angelika Gloeckner-Rist, Dr. Annelies Blom, Prof. Dr. Alexander Danzer, Dr. Achim Schmillen, Dr. Dana Unger, Miriam Frey,

Dr. Elena Simonchuk, Dr. Olga Kutsenko, and Prof. Dr. Irena Kogan. It has been a great pleasure to exchange knowledge and ideas with these scholars.

Finally, I would like to thank Dr. Barbara Dietz who always encouraged my professional development and supported me during the most difficult last stage of the work. Her inspiring sense of humor is gratefully appreciated and her helpful comments on my text led to many useful improvements.

LIST OF ABBREVIATIONS

ESS	European Social Survey
ISJP	International Social Justice Project
IS NASU	Institute of Sociology of the National Academy of Sciences of Ukraine
ISSP	International Social Survey Programme
Marg. effects	Marginal effects
N	Sample size
SOEP	Socio-Economic Panel
Std. Dev.	Standard Deviation
Std. Err.	Standard Error
WVS	World Values Survey

CHAPTER ONE

INTRODUCTION

Ever since man first applied a work tool to produce an object, mankind has striven to create an ever-greater amount of material wealth so as to make life more comfortable and secure. Together with the production of goods, especially those which resulted from collective work and application of labor division, the question of how to fairly distribute the final products among people involved (as well as not involved) in the production process arose, or, in other words: According to what rules should the resources be allocated to individuals or groups? This question led people to reflections on the nature of distributive justice, which is an important component of a more general idea of social justice. Distributive justice treats a particular type of human relationships, namely, those that define how the benefits and costs of people's activities should be distributed among them.

Nowadays it is widely acknowledged that practically all major spheres of social life are greatly affected by the ideas of distributive justice. In modern democratic societies, governmental programs implementing policies that concern people's access to some kind of goods, services, social positions, privileges, etc., are based on a number of normative rules that are supposed to reflect the diversity of principles of distributive justice that are publicly accepted and recorded in laws. Some of the distributive mechanisms are regulated less formally and depend not only on legislation but also on the personal sense of justice inherent to people involved. Wage negotiations, definition of pensions or assessment of tax rates are a few examples of the typical situations in which distributive justice rules play a crucial role.

Research on distributive justice within the social sciences aims to explain a wide range of social phenomena and processes related to justice issues, such as, for example, actual social inequalities, different kinds of discrimination or inclination to protest actions. In order to explain individual actions and social changes resulting from them, scientists refer to people's justice attitudes.

The focus of the present study is on income justice attitudes in Ukraine, a post-Soviet EU-neighboring state located in the Eastern Europe. While a large body of sociological research examines distributive justice attitudes in Western industrialized democracies, much less is known about justice perception in the post-Soviet states. At the same time, there are many factors that make this region particularly compelling and ripe for studying justice attitudes.

Over the last two decades, massive social transformations have taken place in Ukraine. Dictatorship of the communist party was overcome and new democratic institutions appeared, the new direction of development towards European integration was proclaimed and the centrally planned economy was replaced by the capitalist market regulations. Through multiple reforms, including the reforms of distributive system, a new social environment has been created in Ukrainian society. The implementation of complex reforms was accompanied by abundant social, political and economic problems, such as growing income inequalities, widespread informal economic practices, different sorts of discrimination, weakness of the legal system, social insecurity of citizens and more. The new social conditions emerging as a result of transformation of social institutions provide a unique opportunity to study the link between changing patterns of income inequalities and popular justice attitudes. Understanding the changes of people's justice attitudes in times of transformation helps to understand the transformation itself: "Given that behavior is often strongly conditioned by 'what is perceived' rather than 'what actually exists,' the subjective domain is clearly important in understanding the social transformations in the postcommunist societies" (Alwin, Gornev, Khakhulina 1995: 112).

In the last two decades, several comparative justice studies (e.g., ISJP, ISSP) were conducted in Western capitalist democracies and newly independent states of Central and Eastern Europe to explore the differences in justice perception over the countries with different welfare systems and democratic experiences. This was an important step towards general exploration of justice issues for post-communist countries and a great contribution into the comparative justice research. Ukraine had not participated in large national or international studies on distributive justice issues until 2009, at which time the data collection for the present study took place followed by the first implementation of the ISSP survey on social inequality.

The scarce empirical data and unsatisfactory theoretical elaborations prevented comprehensive studying, understanding and explaining many social phenomena and processes related to distributive justice issues in

Ukraine until now. As a result, the field of distributive justice in Ukraine currently remains almost completely unexplored. The scientific community of post-Soviet countries, having practically no tradition of empirical social research, generally paid little attention to and did not advance much in studying the distributive justice issues in the first two decades after the collapse of the Soviet Union. There are single attempts of empirical research on social inequality and justice problems, however, shortcomings in methodology and mostly descriptive character of reported results point to overall underdevelopment of this field of study. My study aims to fill this gap through detailed examination of distributive justice attitudes of Ukrainian citizens.

In the remainder of the introduction, I clarify three important questions related to the present study: Why is it important to examine the justice attitudes of people and what reasons motivate this research? What are the key concepts to be used in this study? And which methodology should be applied in order to answer the research questions?

1.1 Importance of studying distributive justice

People's justice attitudes and beliefs have multiple implications for a wide range of social phenomena at the societal (macro level), organizational (meso level) and individual level (micro level).

As far as the macro level is concerned, scholars stress among the reasons to study the contrast between reality and justice attitudes of people the suggestion that ideas about what is just figure among the factors that shape the actual distributions of rewards (e.g., Jasso, Webster 1999: 368). Social scientists argue that individual beliefs and ideologies form a feedback for the structural characteristics of societies. A certain level of consensus regarding social and especially distributive justice is one of the premises for achieving legitimacy and stability of political systems (Kluegel, Mason 2004). Discrepancies between justice attitudes across different social groups may lead to growth of the conflict potential and result in confrontation actions, protests, revolutions and overall destabilization of social system. Social change and stability of established order are affected by people's justice attitudes. The history of the world has shown that different kinds of social inequalities that result from an unequal distribution of income, status positions, life chances and other goods persist in a society until they are legitimized by the population. Purposive actions aimed at changing the structure of inequalities take place when people realize that the distribution of goods may be organized in another, more effective or more beneficial way for them. Accordingly, the degree to which social inequalities are accepted and approved by the population at the micro level is one of the reasons for changes in the structure of social inequalities at the macro level. This is realized through different mechanisms. For example, it is generally acknowledged that beliefs about social justice play an essential role in people's political behavior. If some people think that income differences in a society are too large (and consequently the distribution of income is unjust), they are likely to vote for left-leaning political parties that force income redistribution (Hadler 2005).

The consequences of justice attitudes may be perceived not only at the macro level. At the meso level of organizations and institutions, justice considerations affect the actions and attitudes of people in many respects. Recent empirical studies have established the effect of distributive justice perceptions on the organizational commitment (Clay-Warner, Hegtvedt, Roman 2005) and have confirmed a strong positive relationship between perception of distributive justice and such phenomena as job satisfaction, trust in management, and lower turnover intention of employees (Choi 2011, Cohen-Charash, Spector 2001). S. Liebig (2002a) studying the case of German metallurgical enterprises provides convincing empirical evidence for the importance of justice attitudes of employees to the effective solution of many managerial problems in organizations. The striking example for the real consequences of people's justice perception is described in an experimental study of J. Greenberg (1990), which revealed the "hidden cost of pay cuts." Greenberg studied the effect of the temporary pay cuts on the rate of employees' theft in two enterprises and found out that in both of them, the level of pilfering at work increased after the pay cuts were implemented. Moreover, the effect was stronger at the enterprise where the reasons for such pay cuts were not explained in comparison to the one where employees got detailed explanation of the necessity of this step. Interestingly, the level of theft withdrew to its initial point as the pay returned to its previous level. One may conclude that the reaction of employees was determined by their expectations of relevant compensation for their work and under conditions of not receiving the full pay, people tried to attain the missing portion of their payment by other means. This study shows that the attitudes towards income justice (which refers to the expected level of compensation) as well as procedural justice (which, in this case, is associated with the presence or absence of explanation for the pay cuts) both affected people's reactions.

Behaviorally oriented social scientists following G. Homans (1961) stressed the significance of justice issues at the micro level of a single individual as well. They regarded justice considerations and evaluations as something one should examine and understand because they can affect person's actions and feelings. Diverse findings point out that individual's justice attitudes tend to be related to subjective perception of the quality of life. For example, empirical studies determine that justice matters are highly relevant for personal happiness, as far as perceived fairness of income inequality in a country is an essential predictor of people's life and job satisfaction (Scher 1997, Oishi, Kesebir, Diener 2011, Sauer, Valet 2013). In addition, a number of studies demonstrated a negative effect of perceived injustice on individual health (e.g., Kivimäki et al. 2003; Spell, Arnold 2007; Bezrukova, Spell, Perry 2010).

Scholars, investigating the link between injustice perception and actions that are motivated by it, state that not every instance of a person desires to have justice restored is followed by appropriate action. Jasso (1986) differentiates between two types of behavior that may follow a justice evaluation: responsive and purposive behavior. The responsive behavior is not aimed at changing the magnitude of injustice perceived. On the contrary, the purposive behavior is designed to alter the unjust situation. The primary interest of the social sciences is directed to the conditions that lead to purposive actions, which are the micro elements of any social situation at the macro and meso levels. Social psychologists argue that if the explanation a person finds for the differential allocation of goods is considered justified (a standard that is acquired through socialization), then the sense of injustice will be muted, even though a person may feel deprived; but, if there will be no excuse found for the violation, the person is likely to desire to restore justice (Karniol, Miller 1981: 81).

One of cases in which individuals are very likely to act in order to restore justice was described by A. deCarufel (1981). The author argued that perceived injustice, accompanied by collective deprivation, may serve as a precondition of a group action. He introduces a term of "fraternal deprivation" to denote a shared perception of group members that one's group was deprived relative to the level of outcomes they felt they deserved (deCarufel 1981: 326). The perception of subjective deprivation of a large number of group members is not enough for the raise of "fraternal deprivation"; the crucial point is the perception of "common fate," which is expressed in belief that other group members are also deprived and which leads to the development of group cohesiveness. After a group has received a potential to act, a triggering event should occur to lead to a collective action. One such triggering event is a sudden shortage of potential resources, which often serves as an incentive for protest and sometimes leads even to violent actions. A provocative action may also serve as a precipitating event. The group deprivation is likely to appear if the group members compare themselves to other groups with respect to resources available to them. This shared perception of being deprived is likely to develop more quickly in groups in which communication networks among members are more sophisticated.

Summing up, the investigations of justice attitudes and beliefs are not only of scientific interest but are related to many practical issues and may be applied in diverse spheres. Comprehensive empirical studies of justice attitudes provide important information for managers' and policymakers' decisions as far as such studies help to detect the signals for inconsistencies between people's aspirations and actual state of affairs and to predict the success of potential decision implementations.

1.2 Justice perception, attitudes, judgments and beliefs

Justice perception, attitudes, judgments and beliefs are terms I often use in this study. It is common in the social sciences for there to be no unique definition and understanding of such abstract notions. The mentioned notions are not exceptional. Therefore, different scholars use them in different manners and argue about the application of each of them in different contexts, trying to identify the subtle distinctions between these terms. To avoid ambiguity in the meaning of these concepts when using them in this study, I find it useful to specify their content and in this way to clearly indicate the logic of their application.

It is widely acknowledged that injustice occurs if there is a discrepancy between desirability of a person's fate and that to which this person is entitled. In terms of distributive justice, this means that justice is when each person gets his or her due. What is considered as "due" may vary across different conceptions of justice and, hence, across different people, who evaluate a given situation. Political philosophers in their theoretical speculations on social justice argue that the crucial role in deciding on what is just belongs to the general moral principles commonly applied by people in judging on justice. Recent empirical studies provide exhaustive evidence on the existence of such "standards," "principles," or "normative frameworks" that guide respondents' judgments concerning justice of income distribution. Scholars have provided a great amount of literature illustrating application of justice principles under different circumstances in various societies. A specific nature of the justice principles applied in a concrete society is a core question of the majority of distributive justice studies and an important issue in understanding the actual social inequalities. According to a philosophical normative perspective, such justice principles take the form of intrinsic moral constructions and norms that guide a person's understanding of justice and provide a basis for justice attitudes and beliefs.

The concept of attitudes is rather psychological in nature. This notion describes an evaluative response towards an object or a situation. According to the literature in social psychology, attitudes encompass affective, behavioral and cognitive responses (Bohner, Wänke 2009). For example, an employer may strongly believe that the effort of his workers should be rewarded, because it motivates them to work better (cognitive), he may become happy if the employees are completely devoted to their work (affective), and he may pay higher wages to those who perform better (behavioral). The attitudes may consist entirely from one of these three elements or be inseparably presented by all of them at once. Therefore, it is reasonable to consider attitudes as a summary evaluation of any object or situation. Justice attitudes are subjective phenomena that similarly to justice perceptions on a higher level of generalization provide a substantive aggregate, namely, a normative framework for making justice judgments. Justice attitudes may sometimes be outcomes of justice perception; sometimes vice versa they affect the subjective perception of justice. Attitudes as subjective mental properties are more stable than opinions, however, they are less constant than beliefs.

Beliefs of an individual are stable mental coherent structures that deal with an understanding of phenomena and processes, and relate to how people define and regard them. J. Rydgren (2011: 73) suggests that there are generally six types of the belief formation processes: by observation, by relying on information received from others (including socialization), by inferences that go beyond direct observation, using inductive strategies, by deduction from other beliefs, by adapting beliefs to fit desires (wishful thinking), and by dissonance-reducing mechanisms. Understanding the beliefs' formational mechanisms helps to explain apparent beliefs and to understand people's actions that are motivated by them.

Perceptions relate to how a person observes and perceives reality. Perceptions are ordinarily marked by individual values and cultural environments and therefore do not necessarily reflect the actual state of affairs but the subjective picture of reality in the mind of observer. Generally speaking, any kind of perception is subjective by its nature; however, taken together, perceptions are likely to show some degree of commonality. This happens primarily because, within a society, individuals' perceptions are formed under the same reference points, that is, the context or environment constituted by specific social, economic, political and cultural conditions. Therefore, people living in the same social system are naturally inclined to analogous opinions or ideas. Justice perception of a single person shows how this person regards the reality from the justice perspective. Prevailing justice perceptions of a society may be conceived as a snapshot capturing the "average" justice perceptions of its people. In this sense, justice perception is a general picture that can be derived from studying the justice attitudes, beliefs, and judgments spread in a society. Perception of social justice forms a basis for justice attitudes and judgments but simultaneously is affected by them. What people consider just or unjust is reflected in their subjective perception of the situation and may result in real actions of these people. This regularity was summarized in the Thomas-Theorem: "If men define situations as real, they are real in their consequences" (Esser 1999: 63).

Justice judgments are manifestations of the sense of justice. They consist of evaluative and emotional components. It is often assumed that justice judgments result from the application of justice principles to a concrete situation or case, however, the process of formulating a judgment involves a mixture of different elements such as individual's values, understanding of situation, style of expression and personal preferences. Therefore, it is useful to remember that judgments may equally be the result of the expression of beliefs and attitudes as well as the reaction on the external circumstances. To evaluate justice or to judge on it means to put a value on some object, action or situation and to place this object, action or situation in an ordering (ranking). The judgmental process occurs at a preconscious level and is revealed indirectly in the person's reactions to a given event (Lerner 1981: 13). I use the terms "justice evaluations" and "justice judgments" in the following text synonymously.

1.3 Methodological approach of analytical sociology

Modern social science has accumulated plenty of ways to conduct social research, and the methods to acquire new knowledge are abundant. This diversity yet arouses uncertainty, tensions and discussions among the representatives of "opposite" "non-complementary" approaches. Many leading European and American sociologists (e.g., P. Hedström 2005, A. B. Sørensen 1998, J. Coleman 1986) have subjected to criticism the divergent tendency of social theory and empirical research, which reflected how social research may be performed in two extreme ways. On the one hand, a so-called variable-sociology is considered to be an overly instrumental approach to the investigation of social reality producing numerous descriptions and employing routine tests of parochial correlations. On the other hand, general social theories are not appropriate for being empirically tested and discussing the social macro phenomena without providing the mechanisms linking them to the micro level. Both approaches poorly contribute to understanding and explaining social phenomena. The critics suggest that "a path must be hewn between the eclectic empiricism of variable-based sociology and often vacuous writings of the 'grand' social theorists" (Hedström 2005) and propose an alternative approach in sociologically meaningful middle-range theories that provide explanatory mechanisms for various social phenomena. This approach to sociological theorizing and research is called analytical sociology (Hedström 2005, Hedström, Bearman 2011) and is gradually becoming more influential in empirical social research (examples of the studies using the analytical sociology approach: Petersen 1992, Hedström, Åberg 2005, Auspurg 2010, Polavieja 2012, Young, Weerman 2013). Among others, K. Auspurg (2010) applies the approach of analytical sociology in several empirical studies on social inequalities including a study of people's distributive justice attitudes.

The core concern of analytical sociology is explanation. Unlike descriptions that seek answers to "what" and "which" questions, the explanation deals with "why" and "how" questions. According to J. Elster, to explain an event is to give an account of why it happened (Elster 2010: 9), or, in other words, to explain why we observe what we observe, why some social phenomena change over time or why and how different social phenomena are interrelated in space and time.

Among three different types of explanation – deductive-nomological, statistical and mechanism-based – analytical sociology considers the latter as the most appropriate for the social science (Hedström 2005: 33). R. Boudon suggests that a "social mechanism" is the well-articulated set of causes responsible for a given social phenomenon and the ultimate causes have the character of being individual decisions (Boudon 1998). In compliance with this statement, P. Hedström and P. Bearman (2011: 8) argue that the basic explanatory principle behind the mechanism approach is that proper explanation identifies the entities, activities, and relations that jointly produce the collective outcome to be explained. Application of this idea to the explanation of social phenomena implies structural individualism. This methodological paradigm assigns a unique explanatory role to individual's actions and differs from traditional methodological individualism only by emphasizing the effect of the social structures that constitute social environment for individuals' actions on these actions. Social structures are, in turn, explainable as the outcomes of individual actions. Summing up, the structural individualism refers to the idea of explanation of macro phenomena by addressing the micro level of individual actions that are structured by the situations in which individuals act (Esser 1999: 27).

According to one of the most outstanding representatives of the outlined approach P. Hedström (2005), the distinctive features of the analytical sociology are as follows:

1. Explanation. Middle-range theories[1] should provide mechanisms that form a basis for understanding of why we observe social phenomena that we observe.

2. Dissection and abstraction. In order to analyze a social phenomenon, the first step is to it into its constituent elements, which are entities and activities. The most essential elements should then been brought into focus.

3. Precision and clarity of theories and notions. Vague and ambiguous notions and ideas should be avoided in order to explain the social phenomena by developing a mechanism-based explanation. R. Boudon called such terms "black boxes," which are concepts that only seem to explain a social phenomenon but which in fact are not its final causes. These terms are actually in need of analysis and decomposition themselves.

4. Focus on actions. Explaining actions of concrete individuals on a micro level is an intermediate and central step in the explanatory strategy that will further lead to the explanation of a social phenomenon under consideration.

To outline the idea of my research in the context of analytical paradigms, I refer to the basic model of the logic of explanation developed and discussed in the writings of R. Boudon (1998), J. Coleman (1986, 1994), J. Elster (2010), H. Esser[2] (1993, 1999), P. Hedström (2005), T. Schelling (1978), and others.

Following J. Coleman (1994), P. Hedström, R. Swedberg (1998) and H. Esser (1999, 1993), figure 1.1 displays the basic model of sociological

---

[1] This notion is understood in terms of R. Merton approach. More on middle-range theories can be found in Merton (1967).

[2] One of the most detailed and thorough descriptions of the logic of explanation in terms of analytical sociology paradigm is provided by a modern German sociologist Hartmut Esser, who stresses the importance and status of mechanism-based explanation in the social sciences in his works "Sociology: general fundamentals" (Esser 1999) and "Sociology: special fundamentals." Vol. 1 (Esser 1993).

explanation. This scheme is also called macro-micro-macro model, because it links the two observable macro phenomena via micro level of individuals' actions. As Figure 1.1 demonstrates, social situation 1 is considered to be a cause of the social situation 2, which is in fact the social outcome a researcher intends to explain. Each of the arrows (a, b, and c) indicates the type of a mechanism in sociological explanation: a) refers to situational mechanisms, b) – to action-formation or behavioral mechanisms, and c) – to transformational mechanisms.

Figure 1.1 Basic model of sociological explanation

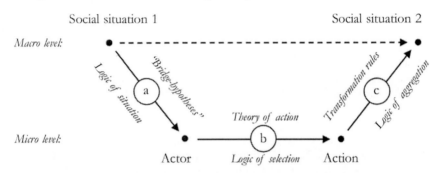

This scheme implies that to explain a social phenomenon (social situation 2), a researcher has to uncover three different mechanisms that describe respectively how social environment influences individuals and forms their beliefs, expectations and judgments (a), how individuals make decisions and select their actions (b), and why acting as they do, they bring about the social phenomenon a researcher intends to explain (c).

The first step of the explanation is reconstruction of the social situation, which an actor believes (s)he is confronted with. The micro-level construct "actor" is understood as a system of individual's subjective beliefs, expectations, and judgments. They are defined by both external and internal conditions, which make up objective and subjective framework of individual actions. This special kind of association between the macro and micro level is called "logic of the situation," and it is reconstructed in descriptions of social conditions by use of the so-called "bridge-hypotheses" (Esser 1993: 94) that describe the constructs of the "first order": individual perceptions of the situation. Situational mechanisms explain how specific macro level situations affect individual attitudes, values, expectations and judgments.

The second step of explanation located on the micro level is described by the logic of selection, which is concerned with individual desires/interests, beliefs, motives and action opportunities/restrictions that generate a certain action. In this stage, theories of action (such as DBO theory (Hedström 2005), "Wert-Erwartungstheorie" (Esser 1993, 1999), diverse applications of rational choice and game theories, etc.) are of fundamental importance for the explanation of individual actions.

The link between micro level of actions and macro level of the resulting social situation forms the last third step of the basic explanation scheme and is called the logic of aggregation. It is described by the aggregative transformation of the consequences of individual actions. This is one of the most complicated link of the explanation, because, as T. Schelling suggests, the "situations, in which people's behavior or people's choices depend on the behavior or the choices of other people, are the ones that usually don't permit any simple summation or extrapolation of the aggregates. To make that connection we usually have to look at the *system of interaction* between individuals and their environment, that is, between individuals and other individuals and the collectivity" (Schelling 1978: 14). This means that the general and formal rules of aggregation, which links the microlevel of individual's actions to the macrolevel of social phenomena, should primarily take into account the nature of the individuals' interrelations. The logic of aggregation could be expressed in the form of special transformational mechanisms (e.g., Schelling's tipping model (Schelling 1978), models of the classic game theory, neoclassical market models, models of collective behavior (Granovetter, Soong 1983, Hedström 1994) etc.). Analyzing social phenomena as outcomes of the actions of interacting people implies agent-based modeling – a theoretical tool used to assess how diverse action logics and interaction structures bring about social phenomena of different kind. The first two stages of the explanation scheme (figure 1.1, arrows *a* and *b*) often belong to the focuses of empirical quantitative research, but the third one traditionally constitutes the domain of pure theorizing. However, Y. Åberg and P. Hedström demonstrate how agent-based modeling may be combined fruitfully with quantitative research in their study on transition out of unemployment (Hedström, Åberg 2005).

To sum up, the central task of social research according to the analytical sociology approach is to explain the social outcomes of individuals' actions. The typical research questions that imply the explanation of social outcomes explicitly interesting for the social science may, for example, be formulated as follows: Why do people evade paying taxes? Why do women receive lower wages than men for the same jobs? Why does everyday corruption flourish in the post-Soviet countries? Tax evasion, gender wage gap or corruption are all the macro level phenomena that a researcher may seek to explain. The common issue of all these phenomena is that they are all related, to some extent, to the distributive justice beliefs of people. If people believe that paying taxes does not contribute to their common wealth and that injustice occurs when the state takes away their "honestly earned money," they are going to avoid paying taxes even under the risk of being punished. If people are convinced that female workers deserve less money for their job than their male counterparts do, they will pay smaller wages to women. If people can justify their taking bribes for the services they are supposed and empowered to provide, they are likely to be corrupt. Each of these cases has many nuances that can be accounted for only in thorough analysis of the three types of mechanisms: situational, behavioral and transformational. Nevertheless, the role of justice attitudes and beliefs has an essential importance for the explanation of these social outcomes as one of the basic elements of the micro level. R. Boudon argued that "Analyzing social mechanisms requires – at least ideally – making them the outcomes of the individual beliefs, actions, attitudes, and so on. Consequently, a final account of a social mechanism is reached when these beliefs, actions, and attitudes can themselves been explained" (Boudon 1998: 199). I can rephrase and summarize this idea as follows: in order to explain social outcomes, we have to explain people's actions. To do so, we need to take people's attitudes and beliefs into account. This implies that we first need to explain how people's attitudes and beliefs are formed and shaped by the social context in which people are embedded.

Distributive justice attitudes and beliefs in Ukraine are the subject of explanation in this study. My present research focuses on the first explanation step of the basic model and systematically explores the situational mechanisms that bring about distributive justice attitudes and beliefs of Ukrainian citizens. This study does not claim to go beyond this purpose and to ultimately explain any macro level phenomenon caused by the people's actions motivated by the justice beliefs, nor does it claim to provide an account for selection and execution of such actions. This study seeks to form a solid ground for further research on these and other questions by explaining the structural impact of the social situation on the formation of actual distributive justice attitudes in Ukraine.

Taking into account the absence of any empirical information on the character of justice principles that rule people's judgment of just incomes in Ukraine, I am entering to some extent terra incognita by formulating and testing the bridge-hypotheses about the influence of the social context on the justice attitudes of Ukrainians. The aim of this study is to clarify the way people perceive and understand distributive justice in Ukrainian society and to shed light on the principles actually applied by people while defining just incomes. Hence, the central question I am answering in this work is this: Why do Ukrainians have the justice attitudes they have?

To understand and explain the justice attitudes of Ukrainians comprehensively, it is necessary to consider them from two complementary perspectives. First is the perspective "from inside," which implies that the formation of justice attitudes is analyzed in the context of the current social situation in Ukraine. The second perspective is "from outside," which stresses some important features of the justice attitudes in Ukraine by comparing them with justice attitudes in another country providing a different context of social institutions to its citizens.

The perspective of inside presupposes focus on shared beliefs and attitudes of people as well as comparison of these beliefs and attitudes across population groups within the society. On the other hand, some of the apparent saliencies of justice attitudes that result from the difference of social structures in which people are embedded can be captured better if one refers additionally to the social structure and justice attitudes in a reference society. This means that some of hypotheses derived from the adaptation and other theories may be tested only through comparative analysis. Thus, my research strategy employs two investigation approaches, which I call contextual and comparative perspectives.

Seeking an answer for the central research question of this study from the contextual perspective implies treatment of the following questions: Does a normative structure for making judgments about income distribution justice exist in Ukraine? Which income inequalities are considered just/unjust by the people? Which justice principles prevail while judging the just incomes? How much consensus about the justice principles exists in Ukrainian society among various social groups? In order to provide answers to these questions, a well-founded theoretical background as well as a thorough analysis of the social processes related to structural transformation in post-Soviet Ukraine is needed.

The comparative perspective of the present study deals with an analysis of institutional differences and their effect on the justice attitudes within two different societies. As a reference country, the case of Germany is considered. This country seems to be an appropriate point of reference for at least two reasons. First, as far as the independent Ukraine proclaimed democratization as the primary goal of its political development and officially declared an intention to pursue the course of European integration, it is particularly interesting to assess the disparities in justice attitudes present in Ukraine (a post-Soviet transforming society) and Germany (one of the most developed capitalist European countries).

The second reason is that recent German sociological research provides several state-of-the-art empirical studies investigating justice attitudes of citizens. The availability of this important empirical material allows for testing the diverse effects of institutional environment on the people's justice attitudes and consequently helps to present more sophisticated analysis of income justice perception in Ukraine. The principal questions within the comparative perspective of my study are as follows: How are people's attitudes concerning principles of just earnings' distribution shaped by the social structure of society? What are the main differences in distributive justice perception in Ukraine and Germany? What are the determinants of the apparent differences?

1.4 Plan of the study

In order to answer the research questions posed above and to examine the complex field of distributive justice attitudes in Ukraine, the following chapters present a set of steps for empirical social research.

In chapter two, "Normative theories of distributive justice," I begin with a brief discussion of the philosophical-normative and empirically oriented social science traditions in the social justice studies and present an overview of the most salient theoretical approaches in this field. By discussing and ordering the diverse philosophical approaches to the idea of distributive justice, my intention is not to contribute to the elaboration of some new taxonomy or provide a comprehensive analysis of the philosophical idea of social justice but rather to give a systematic and brief insight into the long tradition of the development of the distributive justice concept as well as to stress the ideas that form the theoretical background of my study. I draw upon some of the relevant theories of political philosophy and provide arguments in favor of multiprinciple justice approach, which forms the basic part of the theoretical framework in my research. The concluding part of this chapter summarizes some of the most important elements of the justice theories reviewed, namely those statements that constitute a point of departure for my empirical analysis.

Contrary to many scholars, I believe that normative philosophical approach in justice studies and empirically oriented social research in this field can be fruitfully combined and benefit one another. At the same time, though the understanding of the justice concept in political philosophy is an important component of the present research, it should be understood that this work is an example of empirical justice study and therefore special attention is paid to empirical findings of the social science. Thus, in the third chapter, "Empirical distributive justice research," I proceed with a review of the recent empirical studies of the justice attitudes and beliefs. Special focus is turned to the social justice research in post-Soviet states. Apart from the research questions and recent findings of the distributive justice studies, I consider the methods applied for examining the justice attitudes, beliefs and judgments including classic approach of attitudes measurement and innovative technique of factorial survey. The factorial survey method was developed by P. Rossi to capture and assess the influence of multiple factors on the dependent variable separately, which, as a rule, measures a specific kind of attitudes, norms or beliefs. After presenting the method, I discuss its advantages and disadvantages and briefly identify the reasons for the choice of factorial survey design as a method for data collection in my study.

In the fourth chapter, "Middle range theories and the explanation of justice attitudes," I review a number of theories that are useful for hypotheses formulation. These theories encompass the following: human capital theory, labor market theory, rational choice theory, socialization theory, theory of cognitive dissonance and some others. The essential statements of these theories are taken as a point of departure to form general propositions about justice attitudes formation.

Chapter five, "Ukrainian context," provides background information on the current Ukrainian socio-economic situation, real income inequalities, poverty level, and salient features of income distribution process in the country. Additionally, I depict the major characteristics of the educational system and labor market entrance as well as political culture of post-Soviet Ukraine. The concluding section of this chapter combines the information on the specific external conditions of Ukraine as a basis for the belief formation with the general propositions of the rational choice, human capital, socialization, adaptation, labor market and other theories. In this way, I formulate the concrete, empirically testable propositions (hypotheses) that are treated in the following chapters.

The sixth chapter, "Research design of Ukrainian study," presents the research design of an empirical study conducted in Ukraine in 2009. The factorial survey method was applied to attain the dataset of 1799 respondents, which forms a basis for statistical analyses performed in the next chapter. I describe in detail a questionnaire design, pretest and data collection procedure.

Chapter seven, "Contextual perspective: distributive justice evaluations in Ukraine," comprehensively treats the contextual perspective of the empirical analysis of justice attitudes in Ukraine and contains the major part of the research findings. I start with the general description of main results concerning the perceived just and unjust inequalities in Ukraine.

Further, I assess a relative weigh of the factors that represent need, merit and equality justice principles for the respondent's justice evaluations. Moreover, this chapter focuses on more specific aspects of justice perception, including gender-related justice attitudes, balance of justice principles in judgments of Ukrainians, and the degree of consensus regarding justice principles across different population groups. In the last section of the chapter, I assess in absolute terms the just amounts of earnings associated with various occupational positions, individual and family characteristics using the G. Jasso's approach.

The following chapter, "Comparative perspective: justice attitudes in Ukraine and Germany," is devoted to the comparison of justice attitudes in two societies: Ukraine and Germany. The cross-national perspective is applied in the current study to test a hypothesis assuming the shaping effect of actual distributive practices in a particular society on the justice attitudes of the citizens. In this chapter, I explore the extent to which income distribution mechanisms and institutional environment shape people's justice attitudes in the context of different social structures.

In the concluding chapter of the book, I briefly summarize the most important results of my study, discuss possible interpretations of these results and provide a plausible explanation of the most striking findings.

CHAPTER TWO

NORMATIVE THEORIES OF DISTRIBUTIVE JUSTICE

According to the tradition established in the field of distributive justice research, there are two fundamental orientations of study known as the philosophical normative and empirical social science approaches. The normative approach is reflected in political philosophy and aims to specify the situation that "ought to be," that is, to determine the basic principles that should regulate the distribution of goods in a society in terms of either overall distribution of goods, or attribution of a just reward to an individual (Raphael 2001, Baum 2004).

On the other hand, empirical approach deals with "is" conditions and examines existing rules and principles of resource distribution as well as peoples' beliefs and judgments concerning justice of such principles (Sabbagh 2002, Liebig 2001, Elster 1995). One of the central questions in empirical justice research is this: What do people think is just? This approach differs substantially from the philosophical perspective, since it does not understand justice judgments as impartial statements. On the contrary, it recognizes that subjective justice judgments are based on the personal preferences and not necessarily on the ethical (moral) beliefs. The empirical approach shows how people judge justice under different circumstances in various situations, how justice attitudes are formed and the consequences of the justice attitudes for individual behavior. The primary interest of the empirical research tradition is thus people's subjective understanding of justice, which is deemed to be the most relevant for their social behavior.

Some scholars argue that both philosophical normative and empirical social science approaches have something to learn from each other and that the combination of these two traditions in justice research may lead to fruitful results (Liebig 2002b: 77). In my view, the normative justice theories can provide important basis for empirical research. They create a theoretical framework, which, in association with middle-range sociological theories, enables formulation of testable hypotheses. In this chapter, I focus on the most prominent normative justice theories, sketch out their main arguments and ideas and explain my choice of theoretical approach in the current work.

2.1 Macro- and micro-, uni- and multidimensional theories of social justice

The basic ideals of distributive justice were changing over course of history. The modern field of distributive justice studies includes a rich diversity of different theories related to either micro- or macrojustice principles. The microjustice principles are standards that are used as guidelines for judgments of the apportionment of incomes to individuals; the macrojustice principles are conceived as guidelines for the judgments concerning income distribution system as an integrated whole (W. Arts et al. 1991). This is an important criterion to distinguish between justice theories. There could be further criteria to classify the large number of justice theories. In my analysis, I opt for the one proposed by Clara Sabbagh (2002).

Her taxonomy structures the most salient distributive justice theories according to two shared dimensions of content: macro- vs. microjustice principles and the unidimensional vs. multidimensional character of these principles. According to the given approach, a combination of the two dimensions yields four groups of theories of distributive justice: unidimensional macro (the utilitarian approach); multidimensional macro (Rawls' theory of justice); unidimensional micro (desert and equity theories); and multidimensional micro (Miller's theory and multiprinciple approach). There is also a fifth group of theories that combines macro- and microjustice ideas with multidimensional character of justice principles. This group, according to Sabbagh, is identified as "hybrid" theories. In the following outline of normative justice theories, this group of theories is exemplified by the Walzer's and Jasso's distributive justice approaches. As far as drawing on indicated taxonomy allows ordered overview of the justice theories, it is used as a further guiding structure.

2.2 Utilitarianism

Classical utilitarianism[1] was founded in the philosophical works of Jeremy Bentham, James Mill, David Ricardo and John Stuart Mill. Bentham's work "Introduction to the principles of Morals and Legislation"

---

[1] The notion of "utilitarianism", which described Bentham's philosophical doctrine, was popularized ater by John Stuart Mill (Sinclair 1907: 2).

(Bentham 1965) presents the first systematic description and explanation of the general principle of utilitarianism. Bentham sought to formulate a basic principle of political philosophy that could have laid the foundation for society, and he believed he had found such a principle in the idea of utility (Düppen 1996: 95). The most famous formulation of the Bentham's utilitarian principle is comprised in his expression "the greatest good of the greatest number." According to this idea, the rational behavior of people is targeted to the maximization of happiness and avoidance of suffering. Shortly formulated, this central idea of utilitarianism assumes the maximization of utility to be the final purpose of the morals and the basic value of human life. The utility was understood in hedonistic terms as happiness, pleasure and wealth. Latest versions of utilitarianism represented by J. Harsanyi (1976) and R. Hare (1978) interpret the utility in terms of personal preferences, will and desire. Irrespective of different interpretations, the utilitarian principle is central to all versions of utilitarianism and applies to all sorts of utility (Sabbagh 2002).

J. Bentham considered the state to be responsible for the welfare of an individual and regarded every person as having equal rights no matter which position she occupied in the hierarchy of power and wealth. That is, in calculating overall utility, personal utilities must have equal weight – nobody has any advantage over others. The ideas of utilitarianism were developed in the nineteenth century by economists and became the foundation of the welfare economics of the twentieth century (Rescher 1966: 11ff).

The utilitarian approach belongs to the unidimensional macrojustice theories as it is based on one universal principle that refers to the whole society rather than to a concrete individual. According to the ethical system of utilitarianism, the principle of the maximization of utility is argued to be the determinant of the just distribution of social resources among the members of a society. Hence, the appropriateness of the concrete mechanisms of distribution is assessed in accordance with their ability to promote the ideal of utility. The overall utility in a society can be measured as a sum of individual utilities or an average utility per person.

Empirical studies within the utilitarian approach develop in several directions. One of them is focused on the search of optimal distribution of goods from the utilitarian point of view. This is typical for the economically oriented welfare studies that attempt to evaluate the efficacy of market mechanisms in terms of the welfare levels in societies as their outcomes (e.g., Arthur, Shaw 1978). Another type of empirical research places emphasis on the conditions under which people prefer the distribution patterns based on the utility principle. One of the classical examples of such research is a study of Frohlich and Oppenheimer (1992), who conducted a number of experiments to test the major assumptions of the most salient justice theories including the utilitarianism (see section 3.1).

2.3 J. Rawls' theory of justice

The normative justice theory of J. Rawls (1972) is undoubtedly one of the most prominent and sophisticated theories of the 20th century. J. Rawls proposed it as a counterbalance to the utilitarian approach, which he was not content with and criticized in his works for taking into account only the total sum of happiness in a society, regardless of its distribution among people. Under these conditions, the infinite maximization of utility of one individual may be regarded as just, even if the rest of individuals at the same time have to suffer.

The justice theory of Rawls refers to the macrojustice multidimensional justice theories and it is founded upon two principles of fair distribution: the first one implies a maximization of equal basic liberties, and the second one (difference principle) justifies unequal distribution of goods if it is realized under the conditions of the equality of opportunity and benefits the least advantaged members of a society. The first principle is considered to be the priority and it should be applied before the second principle can be realized. "Contrary to utilitarianism, it is not enough that inequalities increase the total social good; they must work to the favor of the least advantaged members of society" (Arthur, Shaw 1978: 16).

According to Rawls, these reasonable justice principles are determined by rational individuals in a kind of speculative social contract under the conditions of perfect impartiality. The state of impartiality is achieved when people, though possessing the general knowledge of human nature, economic and societal laws, etc., have no information about their own specific characteristics and position in a society. Rawls called this original position marked by the lack of such information a "veil of ignorance." It is important that people placed behind the "veil of ignorance" determine the justice principles because it creates a situation where people are not able to choose the distributive mechanisms that would benefit them personally at the expense of others rationally. In such a case, preferences for a justice principle are supposed to be guided by ethical considerations rather than by the individual interests. It is clear that the rational individuals are not going to support the unequal distribution of goods, since it would perhaps place them in a disadvantaged position and hinder them from advancement and competition with others on an equal basis.

The realization of justice principles is possible only in the appropriate social context represented by the institutional structure of a democratic society. Since the theory is based on the personal liberty and equality of individuals who agreed on the social contract, it is incompatible with the realities of authoritarian regimes. The idea of social contracts was intentionally recovered by J. Rawls because he attempted to reproduce the environment in which free and rational individuals would agree upon the basic rules to govern the distributions of social goods within their community.

The justice theory of Rawls had a great impact on political philosophy debates and empirical studies of distributive justice. One such study that examined the acceptance of Rawls's distributive justice principles by people in their actual behavior has shown that individuals mostly reject the difference principle (e.g., Frohlich, Oppenheimer 1992).

2.4 Desert principle and equity theory

The idea of desert in the normative philosophical tradition traces back to the works of Aristotle; in empirically oriented social justice studies, it was embodied in the equity principle first introduced into social sciences by G. C. Homans, who suggested that justice could be defined as equality of profit/investment ratio (see Homans 1961).

E. Walster, G. W. Walster and E. Berscheid (1978) in their work "Equity: Theory and Research" argue that every society develops some systems for equitable distribution of rewards among members, but that they differ considerably in what they consider equitable. The scholars promote an idea that: "Groups can maximize collective reward by evolving accepted systems for 'equitably' apportioning rewards and costs among members. Thus, members will evolve such systems of equity and will attempt to induce members to accept and adhere to these systems. Groups will generally reward members who treat others equitably and generally punish members who treat other inequitably" (Walster, Walster, Berscheid 1978: 201). In the real world, this statement seems to be relevant only for the modern democratic liberal societies, since in less developed authoritarian countries, it is often the case that decisions about apportionment of benefits and costs are taken not to maximize collective but individual reward of those who possess access to the public good. Nevertheless, the discrepancy between actual distributive systems and the idea of an equitable just distribution does not diminish the value of the equity theory in general. In addition, the empirical research shows that the desert principle is a universally acknowledged justice principle in very different societies.

In the next paragraphs I will consider two most important approaches related to the equity theory: the equity theory of G. Homans and the status values theory of J. Berger and others.

2.4.1 The equity principle (G. Homans)

George C. Homans developed an approach to distributive justice in the context of his social exchange theory. This approach implies that justice is "a curious mixture of equality within inequality" (Homans, 1961: 244).

In the chapter on justice in "Social behavior. Its elementary forms," Homans introduced three principal interrelated "variables" – profits (rewards), investments and costs. These variables constitute the basis of the justice principle that was called "equity principle". It states: "A man in an exchange relation with another will expect that the rewards of each man be proportional to his costs – the greater the rewards, the greater the costs – and that the net rewards, or profits, of each man be proportional to his investments – the greater the investments, the greater the profits... Finally, when each man is being rewarded by some third party, he will expect the third party, in the distribution of rewards, to maintain this relation between the two of them" (Homans 1961: 232). In other words, Homans claims that people expect a just reward to depend on a person's individual investment and costs, and, at the same time, it should correspond to the level of reward others receive for similar investments and contributions. Homans argued that people, of course, do not measure their rewards and costs exclusively in monetary form or in concrete figures, but they are able to put the objects (positions, activities, persons, etc.) in a rank-order of rewards and costs. Distributive justice, accordingly, assumes that the orders of costs and investments correspond to the order of rewards.

The equity principle regards distributive justice as a relative phenomenon that implies the existence of another person or group as a reference point for comparison. The assessment of justice or injustice is, thus, a result of comparison of investments, costs and rewards across different individuals or groups.

The equity principle goes in line with the rational choice theory in assuming that people who are aware of their interests may interpret the costs and investments in different terms; as a rule, in terms that make the distribution of rewards the most profitable for them. As a consequence, such given characteristics as sex, age, and race may in a specific context also have a meaning of "investment." Homans concludes, that "men certainly assess their own investments and income, but to make a rule of justice work they must assess those of others on the same scale" (Homans 1961: 247). From his point of view, there are no just societies, but rather societies that are more or less just, and the degree of justice depends on the agreement of people on the rules of evaluation and the maintenance of the rough proportionality between investment and reward.

2.4.2 The status value theory (J. Berger)

Another salient approach within the unidimentional microjustice theories known as the status value theory was developed by a group of social scientists led by J. Berger (see Berger et al. 1972). Contrary to the equity principle of Homans, the status value theory focuses on the status significance of rewards rather than on their exchange value. Sociologists criticized the approach of exchange theory for neglecting the structural aspects of distributive justice, which were understood as "the process by which, independently of the comparison of the individual with another, meaning is given to rewards and expectations are formed about their allocation" (Berger et al. 1972: 119). Berger et al. argued that it is not enough to compare two rewards locally; one should also refer to the knowledge of relevant rewards in a generalized referential group [2]. Following the logic of the argument, if the proportion of inputs and outputs is perfectly maintained in a situation of comparison between two employees, it does not mean that their rewards are just. They may both be unjustly under- or overpaid.

Referential comparison is distinguished by the presence of a stable frame of reference, which provides a kind of standard by which the local comparisons acquire meaning. According to the status value theory, the referential structure must have three fundamental properties: it should be unitary, differentiated and balanced (Berger et al. 1972: 134). The referential structure consists of beliefs about the actual state of affairs (what is), and it constitutes a point of departure for the expectations about the just rewards (what ought to be). Persons similar in terms of socially defined valued characteristics expect to be similarly rewarded, otherwise their expectations are violated and injustice occurs. In other words, status value theory defines the situation as unjust if the level of goal-object (reward) of an individual differs from a level of goal-object received by a generalized "other" in a referential structure.

---

[2] Berger et al. (1972) also used the term "generalized objects of orientation."

The authors argued: "A state of distributive justice is always a balanced status situation, while injustice is always an imbalanced status situation. Balanced status situations are stable, imbalanced status situations produce tensions and pressures for change" (Berger et al. 1972: 145). Berger et al. introduced the notions of balanced and imbalanced status situations and distinguished between collective vs. individual and self vs. other imbalance. This distinction is useful because different types of imbalance are associated with different situations of injustice and, according to the authors, lead to different patterns of response to it.

2.5 The multiprinciple approach

Critique of the equity theory has prompted the elaboration of the multiprinciple approach that implied not only self-interest motives of human behavior assumed by the equity theory but also altruistic aspirations of people willing happiness for others. The representatives of the multiprinciple approach recognized multidimensional nature of justice and posited that diverse justice principles may be applied separately or in concert by individuals in different situations. There are three core justice principles that are commonly specified as desert (distribution according to effort, actual contribution or ability of an individual), equality[3] (equal distribution of goods among individuals) and need (distribution according to the level of individual's needs). Sometimes scholars specify additional justice principles, especially when they analyze historically different types of societies. For example, they point out that the principle of ascription (distribution according to person's rights) is one of the most popular justice principles of traditional feudal societies. The general feature of the multiprinciple approach is its pluralistic view of social justice.

2.5.1 D. Miller's theory of justice

David Miller's theory of justice is one of the best-known multiprinciple justice theories. He presented his views in the book "Principles of Social Justice," which presents his attempt to discover the underlying principles used by people while judging some aspect of society as just or unjust and to demonstrate that these principles are coherent when taken separately or together (Miller 1999: ix).

---

[3] The principle of equality states that justice consists in the treatment of individuals as equal. This may sometimes be interpreted not only in terms of rewards but also in terms of chances.

Contrary to many philosophers, D. Miller does not move from intuitive beliefs to highly abstract principles in his work, but rather seeks to find out the practical principles that guide people's justice beliefs. He identifies justice principles that spring from the different modes of relationships between individuals. As such he considers three basic modes of relationships: solidaristic community, instrumental association, and citizenship.

The substantive distributive justice principle within a solidaristic community is a principle of need: "Each member is expected to contribute to relieving the needs of others in proportion to ability" (Miller 1999: 27). The solidaristic community is, as a rule, a relatively small and stable group of people who interact with each other directly, have a similar identity and whose relationships are based on mutual trust and understanding. These can be networks of family members, close friends, but also sometimes religious associations, professional communities, work teams, etc. On the other hand, in the instrumental associations, where each actor interacts with others as an "agent with a set of skills and talents" in order to attain its goals, the appropriate justice principle is distribution according to desert. Finally, the third mode of association Miller touches upon is citizenship. Since in liberal societies each citizen has equal status that defines the scope of liberties, freedoms, rights, and obligations, the central principle of justice in this mode of relationships is considered to be equality: "In their capacity as citizens, people must be treated as equals, and this requires that they enjoy equal legal, political, and social rights" (Miller 1999: 250).

The idea of social justice as portrayed by Miller is deemed to be a criterion for assessment of the basic structures of modern liberal societies. The author seeks to determine the right kind of necessary institutional structures to ensure the distribution of goods according to the justice principles in each of the relevant modes of relationships.

Miller argues that the practical conflict between justice principles arises when the modes of relationships in which people are engaged are defined with some level of uncertainty. This uncertainty is the primary cause of the debates over justice principles to be applied in such ambiguous cases. According to Miller's argument, the clarification of the nature of relationships among people can at least partially resolve this conflict of principles and make people understand what justice demands of them in every single situation of social goods' distribution.

2.6 M. Walzer's theory of justice

Michael Walzer developed a normative justice theory in his monograph "Spheres of Justice" (Walzer 1983). The central notion of Walzer's theory is a so-called complex equality, which establishes a set of relationships that make domination and tyranny not possible: "In formal terms, complex equality means that no citizen's standing in one sphere or with regard to one social good can be undercut by his standing in some other sphere, with regard to some other good" (Walzer 1983: 19). The idea of complex equality is that there are multiple micro and macro justice principles in every society and they should apply in different spheres of distribution where the application of each of them is the most appropriate. According to Walzer, the establishment of a just society is possible only under the conditions of autonomy of such spheres and independence of the unique sets of justice principles applied within each of them.

For example, if one person occupies a better position in the sphere of politics as compared to another person, they are unequal with regard to the distribution of power. However, it should not imply any other inequalities, for example, in spheres of medical care, schooling, access to different services, etc.

Walzer regards three justice principles that appear to "meet requirements of the open-ended principle" (Walzer 1983: 21ff) and are applied in the various distributions of diverse social goods. These are free exchange, desert and need principle. Which principle should be applied in which sphere of distribution is defined by the social meaning of the goods. For example, some of the justice principles that are appropriate for the distribution in sphere of education are not applicable in the same way in the sphere of income distribution, etc. Moreover, more refined distinctions may exist in the same sphere. For example, in primary education, the principle of simple equality is preferred since it ensures all pupils get the necessary basic education. On the other hand, the desert principle is more appropriate in higher education because it helps to match future occupational positions with abilities and interests of students.

The idea of complex equality implies preventing the domination of one social group over another in different spheres of social goods' distributions and facilitates the creation of relative equality in a society. This relative equality presupposes that if one group holds higher rank in some distribution, this should not mean that this group has any advantage in any other distribution of social goods.

2.7 G. Jasso's justice theory

A number of publications recognize the importance of Jasso's justice theory, which combines the principles of macro and microjustice. Contrary to philosophical approaches discussed above, the theory of Jasso has a slightly different focus; it is empirically oriented and is presented in a highly formalized form. The theory describes how individual sentiments of justice are produced. The core issue of this theory is an idea that people subjectively evaluate justice by comparing the actual state of affairs with the ideal state of justice (no matter what justice principles they consider in each of the situations). This relationship applies to any kind of social good that is distributed among people including personal income. The individual justice evaluation of earned income can be expressed quantitatively as a logarithmic function of the ratio of actual earnings to just earnings:

$$justice\ evaluation = \ln \frac{actual\ share}{just\ share}$$

This relationship is called the justice evaluation function and it predicts "the precise magnitude of injustice associated with measured departures from perfect justice in the distribution of earned income" (Jasso 1978: 1398). If the justice evaluation is equal to zero, this corresponds to the situation of perfect justice; the positive segment of values represents unjust overreward, and the negative segment of values represents unjust underreward.

Proceeding from this function, Jasso generated an expression for the true just reward to estimate which information is needed. In order to attain this information, an investigator provides an actual reward to a respondent who should evaluate this reward in terms of justice and provides an expressed justice evaluation. Additionally, the "signature constant," which measures the expressiveness of a respondent, is estimated. By combining these terms in a respective expression (Jasso 2007: 14):

$$just\ reward = A \exp\left(\frac{-J}{\theta}\right)$$

it is possible to rule out the amount of reward, which is considered to be just by people. In this expression A denotes the actual reward, J – the expressed justice evaluation, and θ – the signature constant. Of course, an adequate design of a survey should be used to acquire all needed information and to test the proposed theory. AA factorial survey design is considered to be the most appropriate because it "enables unbiased and consistent estimation of the signature constant theta, and signature constant theta in turn enables estimation of the experienced justice evaluation and the true just reward" (Jasso 2007: 16).

The justice evaluation function together with the factorial survey design was applied in several empirical studies, such as by Shepelak, Alwin (1986); Randall, Mueller (1995); Jasso, Webster (1997, 1999) and brought significant progress in distributive justice research. First of all, application of justice evaluation function confirmed the statement that individuals distinguish different degrees of injustice. This was a telling argument for the development and refinement of the measurement procedures to assess the subjective justice attitudes of people. Moreover, contrary to results coming from analysis of usual abstract item-based survey questions, this approach makes it possible to attain important inferences concerning just rewards in absolute terms.

2.8 Overview

Normative and empirically oriented justice theories approach the distributive justice concept from different perspectives, nevertheless there are some cross-points that create a remarkable potential for the mutual enrichment of these two research traditions. C. Sabbagh (2002) proposed a taxonomy of the most prominent distributive justice theories, which organizes these approaches into five groups. This taxonomy is presented in table 2.1.

Table 2.1 C. Sabbagh's taxonomy of justice theories

	Macrojustice	**Microjustice**
Unidimensional	Utilitarian approach	Equity theory of G. Homans Status value theory of J. Berger
Multidimensional	J. Rawl's theory of justice	Multiprinciple approach (D. Miller)
Hybrid theories		
M. Walzer's and G. Jasso's theories of justice		

The justice theories summarized above have a number of essential elements that are useful for the present research. I would like to name some of them here. This will clarify my theoretical approach and highlight the ideas unfolded in further chapters.

The principles of analytical sociology that constitute the methodology of the present study imply consideration of the subjective justice attitudes of people. As the microlevel of people's attitudes towards the allocation of individual incomes is my principal subject of interest, I refer to the realm of the microjustice principles. In this context, the multiprinciple approach seems the most suitable because it allows for pluralistic nature of justice and does not constrain the choice of advocated justice principle to a single one. Moreover, the multiprinciple theory of justice is known to be empirically oriented. As D. Miller states: "... an adequate theory of justice must pay attention to empirical evidence about how the public at large understands justice, and in particular to the way in which different norms of justice are applied in different social contexts" (Miller 1999: 42). A large bulk of empirical evidence suggests that this approach is the most empirically promising theory of justice and that it can be successfully applied in empirical studies with a focus similar to that of the present study. Some of the recent empirical studies tried to detect the justice principles that guide respondents' judgments concerning justice of income distribution. According to the results of such studies, the existence of multiple standards used by people while judging distributive justice in different situations was confirmed repeatedly (e.g., Jasso, Rossi 1977; Alves, Rossi 1978; Jasso 1994). These findings encourage further investigations in this direction, such as exploring the factors that influence the choice of justice principles to be applied in different situations, studying the conditions under which a trade-off relationship between justice principles appears and examining the impact of individual preferences of justice principles on a person's behavior in different social contexts.

Jasso's theory may be combined very well with the multiprinciple approach. Given that an appropriate data collection technique is used, the application of the respective statements concerning the nature of justice evaluations helps to assess the expressed deviation from the perfect justice. By uncovering the true amount of earnings people consider to be just, it is possible to assess the grade of inconsistency between the outcomes of actual distributive practices and people's expectations.

The elements of the equity theory that imply a comparison of one's earnings with the average income in a reference group are related to the issue of social system effect on the formation of justice perception. This forms another aspect of the present research. Consistent with the status value theory, actual social inequalities are perceived as objectively given through comparison and they are likely to be imprinted in the consciousness of individuals. This may affect their justice judgments and serve as a factor of the social inequalities' legitimation. Further development of this idea leads to the conclusion that a constant reference to the existent level of labor remuneration forms, to an essential extent, the idea of due levels of just rewards among people.

CHAPTER THREE

EMPIRICAL APPROACH IN DISTRIBUTIVE JUSTICE STUDIES

The previous chapter introduced the most salient philosophical conceptions of justice. Social scientists who represent the 'competing' empirical approach in distributive justice research criticize the way of addressing the question "what is just?" applied by political philosophers and consider their widely used methods of introspection and argument as "inappropriate methodology" (Frohlich, Oppenheimer 1992: 1) that fail to uncover the true content of distributive justice. The following sections present methodological, theoretical, and practical aspects of empirical social science research that focus on the problem of distributive justice. Some theoretical considerations outlined in the preceding chapter are developed in further detail and descriptions are provided about how they were tested on empirical data. Further, I present a review of empirical literature on justice attitudes research and its major findings, including key results of international justice studies involving post-communist states and a brief look at the state of post-Soviet justice research within Ukraine.

3.1 Testing the philosophical conceptions

One of the most prominent fundamental studies that brought together grand theory of political philosophy and empirical social science approach was conducted by N. Frohlich and J. A. Oppenheimer (1992), who tried to go beyond "speculation and debate" and find adequate answers to the questions of distributive justice through experimental technique. Based on the quantitative and qualitative data from student samples of three countries (USA, Canada and Poland), they have tested the major assumptions of the utilitarian and Rawls' justice theories. Under the created conditions designed to generate impartial reasoning of participants, they tried to identify the distributive justice principles that were actually applied by individuals in diverse situations.

Contrary to expectations of many thinkers, the most popular principle of distribution among the respondents was neither Rawls' difference principle nor that advocated by utilitarianism, but instead a principle of floor constraint that secures a minimum income for every member of society and does not set any limit at the top of the distribution. In fact, the idea of maximizing the floor income, that is, improving the situation of the least advantaged individual, was the most unpopular justice principle. People mostly supported the statement that the most just distribution of income is the one that maximizes average income in a society only after a certain specified minimum income is guaranteed to everyone. Among 81 groups of experiment participants, 77.8% have chosen this principle as the most just (Frohlich, Oppenheimer 1992: 58ff). The utilitarian principle of maximizing the average income in the society was supported by 12.3%; 8.64% wished to maximize the average income after setting a range constraint (which means that the difference between the poorest and the richest individuals in the society should not exceed a defined amount).

The study of Frohlich and Oppenheimer showed that people are mostly concerned that individuals not fall below a subsistence minimum level. They prefer to guarantee the minimum income for everybody and take into consideration the arguments of the individual's fate and welfare in society. The floor-constraint principle was stably supported in different experiments: in the situation that presupposed impartiality, when individuals were ignorant of their particular position in society and were not able to determine their personal interests, and when their positions were defined and the interests were clear.

The results of this experiment show that people prefer to feel secure and therefore they consider the principle that ensures the satisfaction of their basic needs regardless of their employment situation, position in the social and occupational hierarchy and other objective and subjective circumstances. At the same time, it is not enough to be guided solely by the need principle. Participants of the experiment widely acknowledged that the differentiation of the income according to the principle of desert produces an incentive for people to work better, harder, and more efficiently. This provides support for the pluralistic nature of distributive justice in mind of individuals.

The study of Frohlich and Oppenheimer dealt with testing the macrojustice principles: the purpose of the experiments was to detect the most preferable order in a society that, according to people's beliefs, would assure the most just distribution of welfare. There are some other studies that had a similar macrojustice orientation but focused on the testing of one particular theory of political philosophy. For example, A.

Michelbach et al. (2003) presented an experimental study to test the assumptions of J. Rawls' theory of justice. The design of the experiment was rather complex and perhaps somewhat ambiguous, but the findings of the experiment seem noteworthy. The purpose of the study was to analyze the preferences of respondents [1] for equality or efficiency as guiding principles of the income distribution in an imagined society. Authors tried to reach "strict impartiality" by asking their participants to give advice to a hypothetical society as observers from outside. The task was to rate a number of income distributions that were created by manipulating the three levels (low, medium, high) of two variables: equality and efficiency (Michelbach et al. 2003: 526). Further, authors introduce two other pieces of information. The first concerned the degree to which income was explained by effort and ability as opposed to luck, personal connections, etc. This was a way to study the effect of merit considerations when choosing the most fair income distribution. Second, the need criterion was taken into account by indicating a poverty line in a society. The major finding of this study, in fact, provides support for the multiprinciple justice theory, since the data show that the respondents use the allocation principles simultaneously and consider all mentioned normative criteria of justice: equality, efficiency, need and desert. The authors conclude that a considerable minority behaved "consistent with a Rawlsian maximin strategy." This is in line with the findings of Frohlich and Oppenheimer.

The study of Michelbach et al. synthesizes the normative and empirical traditions of distributive justice research. Its design is advantageous because it allows for the testing of relevance of normative justice principles in the distributive behavior of people eliminating effects of individual social characteristics. This and other similar studies have shown that in order to predict the distributive behavior of people comprehensively, one should consider the conceptions of political philosophy. However, the impartial judgment of justice may only partly explain the justice attitudes and subsequent behavior. Hence, in empirical tradition, the ideas of normative theories are to be combined with the statements of the instrumental theories of the social science. Only this complex approach may provide the most precise and reliable answer to this question: What do people believe is just?

But prior to discussing on the relevant middle-range sociological theories and formulating testable hypotheses for my study, I turn to the experience of empirical sociology in justice attitudes research. In the

---

[1] This study based on a sample of undergraduates from the University of Houston and Texas Southern University.

following section I briefly overview the existing international experience of surveys on distributive justice to depict the current state of justice research and its major findings relevant for my study. I approach this review by focusing on the following questions: What aspects of justice attitudes were studied? What research questions were posed? What measurement techniques were applied?

3.2 Distributive justice attitudes: key findings of empirical studies

One of the research fields that drew considerable attention in empirical literature on social justice is devoted to people's perception of income inequalities and legitimation of existing social systems. The primary focus of this research is on the definition of differences in inequality perception among population groups and the examination of factors that affect such perceptions. Researchers stress the importance of investigating income inequalities perception because it is directly linked to peoples' justice attitudes and hence to their support of certain distributive practices. This is thought to have implications for legitimization of institutions involved into distribution of wealth.

There are several ways in which the redistributive policies can be influenced by the citizens of a democratic state. One of them is through a so-called median voter (Meltzer, Richard 1981, Milanovic 2000). Scholars describing this mechanism proceed from an empirically grounded assumption that preferences for redistribution are linked to individual's level of income. Many studies show that people who are better off accept more income inequality (e.g., Liebig 2007, Hadler 2005, Gijsberts 2002). At the same time, the larger the income inequality in a society is, the lower the relative position of a median voter – an individual with the median level of income – is, and the more he/she has to gain from redistribution (Aristei, Perugini 2010: 182). According to the self-interest assumption of the rational choice theory, people who may gain from redistribution are more likely to support higher taxes on the rich and larger social transfers for the poor. In other words, low-income groups, as a rule, place more emphasis on the equality justice principle than do high-income groups. This statement found empirical support in numerous studies (e.g., Hadler 2005, Aalberg 2003, Gijsberts 2002).

The link between diverse respondents' social and demographic characteristics and attitudes towards income inequality has been examined in many empirical studies and it was discovered that some social groups indeed tolerate more income inequality than do others. For instance,

German sociologist S. Liebig (2007) compares the attitudes towards income inequalities in three population groups of the German society: (1) the unemployed, (2) blue-collar workers and employees with low occupational status, and (3) employees with high occupational status. Analyzing the ISJP and other survey data[2], the author concludes that the highest support of egalitarianism is found among unemployed citizens and the lowest is found among the employees with high occupational status (Liebig 2007). Similarly, M. Forsé and M. Parodi (2007: 517) analyze the cross-national ISSP 1999 data to show that, in general, in addition to people who are better off, men and older persons also accept larger income inequalities in different modern countries[3].

At the same time, social groups that accept more income inequality as a rule favor to a greater degree the principle of desert. For instance, empirical analysis of T. Aalberg (2003) shows that better educated, older people and those with higher income in Western democracies support the equity principle of distribution significantly stronger based on the ISJP 1991. However, in Russia, age has the opposite effect: older people are less supportive of distribution based on desert principle compared to younger citizens (Aalberg 2003: 59). Similarly, the most vulnerable social groups tend to support the principle of need more strongly. This is in line with the findings from the study of M. Alves and P. Rossi who show that "high-status respondents place greater weight on merit considerations, while low-status respondents give need considerations more weight" (Alves, Rossi 1978: 559). In general, empirical studies point to people's tendency to believe that the fairest distributive principle is the one that is most advantageous for them and not the one based on the criterion of impartiality, which was stressed in the works of political philosophers.

To explain the justice preferences of people, many social scientists refer to the classifications of "justice ideologies" (Legewie 2008, Wegener, Lippl, Christoph 2000, Wegener, Liebig 1995, 2000, Liebig 2007). One of the most prominent approaches in this respect is the anthropological paradigm of M. Douglas (1978). It presumes that social environment plays a decisive role in people's understanding of how goods and burdens should be distributed among individuals and distinguishes four types of such social environments as a result of different combinations of levels in two orthogonal dimensions: hierarchy of social structures ("grid") and social incorporation or strength of ties within social entities ("group").

---

[2] The author used the ISJP data coming from three waves of the survey conducted in Germany in 1999, 1996, 2000 and "Arbeit und Fairness 2004" survey data.
[3] The data used in this paper comes from France, USA, Germany, GB, Sweden, Spain, Poland, and Japan.

This yields four justice ideologies: egalitarianism, individualism, ascriptivism and fatalism. Egalitarianism results from a combination of "strong group" and "low grid." In such a social environment, social hierarchy (inequality) is not pronounced and members of the social group share strong solidarity feelings with each other. In the case of individualism, both social hierarchy and group pressure are weak, and success of individual upward social mobility is a matter of his or her personal achievements. Ascriptivism implies strong social hierarchy and strong ties within social groups. Here, individuals form closed communities that are ordered in a social hierarchy. Finally, fatalism is associated with weak group ties and "high grid." In this situation, individuals are dependent on the position they occupy in a social hierarchy but are devoid of solidarity feelings with persons of similar status.

By applying the grid-group theory, social scientists try to understand the determinants for the justice attitudes in a certain social environment. One of the examples of application of the Douglasian paradigm is the study of B. Wegener and S. Liebig (1995, 2000), in which the authors examine and explain the difference in ideological preferences of East and West Germans using the ISJP data. The main purpose of the analysis was "to discover if the differences in justice ideologies may be explained merely through structural effects or if, in addition, there is an East-West effect" (Wegener, Liebig 1995: 277). Using a structural equation modeling approach, the scholars conclude that the social structure characteristics (effects of respondent's social class, job mobility, age and sex) are the key determinants of the ideological discrepancies in the two parts of Germany, and the thesis of additional effect of cultural differences finds not enough empirical support. In other words, it was established that objective characteristics of the social structure play a decisive role in the formation of people's justice attitudes. Summarizing the findings of the reviewed studies, one may conclude that the justice attitudes and beliefs of people are strongly influenced by their individual characteristics as well as by the characteristics of the social environment in which they are embedded.

As far as individual characteristics are concerned, it is remarkable that a relatively large body of literature is devoted to a gender aspect in the perception of justice of earnings. This includes, in particular, a number of studies on persistent differences in justice attitudes between men and women. In general, empirical data analysis confirms that women hold more egalitarian attitudes concerning the just distribution of income than do men (e.g., Lewin-Epstein, Kaplan, Levanon 2003, Aalberg 2003, Wegener, Liebig 2000). Male and female respondents not only differ with respect to their preferences for the justice principles, but they also have generally different attitudes towards income distribution among men and women. Some studies have found or estimated that the gender wage gap is regarded as just by the respondents – a result of double standard applied by respondents in evaluating just reward for men's and women's labor (e.g., Sauer et al. 2009b, Jann 2003, Jasso, Webster 1997, Jasso 1994). These studies report the discrimination of women in ascribing them lower just earnings compared to men ceteris paribus. At the same time, G. Jasso and M. Webster (1999), suggested that the gender gap in just earnings favoring men in the USA, found by these researchers in earlier studies, did not appear in 1999 when they surveyed a sample of students. The authors conclude that irrespective of the actual state of affairs with respect to a gender wage gap in the USA, students do not discriminate against women in the sense of just earnings.

As a further step, scholars sought to determine whether the perceived gender wage gap differs according to the observer's gender and estimated the justice perception of men and women. Their analyses show that assuming equal job and family characteristics of two employees, respondents of both sexes suggest higher incomes to be just for a male employee (Auspurg et al. 2008, Jann 2003). Such discriminating answer patterns are, as a rule, attributed to the socialization effects that lead to the internalization of the traditional gender roles definition and consequently shape justice attitudes. Interestingly, B. Jann (2003) has shown that the "discriminatory" justice attitudes are even more pronounced among women: female respondents ascribed even smaller just incomes to women than did male respondents. Analyzing the just gender wage gap in Germany by using three factorial survey studies, C. Sauer (2014) reveals that the actual income inequalities people are embedded in play essential role for the justice perceptions of respondents. He found that the size of the just gender wage gap was associated with the size of actual earnings inequalities between men and women in respective regions of the country.

In order to explore the strength of effects that various justice principles have on the justice judgments of people, scholars directed their attention to the complex combinations of individual characteristics. Applying the factorial survey desig[4], social scientists determined the relative importance of the job-related and personal characteristics that define the amount of income considered just in different situations. As a matter of fact, people's assessment of the just incomes in Western democracies is primarily defined by occupation (Sauer et al. 2009a, 2009b, Hermkens, Boerman 1989, Alves, Rossi 1978). The hierarchy of occupations, measured as a

---

[4] See section 3.5.2.

rule through occupational prestige, is the strongest predictor of just earnings. Educational attainment, work performance, work experience, job tenure and other factors belong to further important criteria that are attributed to the desert principle of distributive justice and considered by people in their judgments on justice of earnings. Empirical findings suggest that because of the largest effects attributed to job-related characteristics of occupation and educational attainment, the merit criterion plays a crucial role in judging distributive justice.

At the same time, it was assumed that people's justice judgments involve not only the considerations of merit but also those of need. This justice criterion is operationalized in different studies through consideration of age, number of children, marital status, health status, etc., of a vignette person.

The discriminatory attitudes were measured through an introduction of demographic dimensions such as ethnicity, sex, and race. In several cases, scholars additionally tested the effect of institutional characteristics such as economic situation of a firm and firm size on people's justice judgments. These characteristics were considered as factors that define the "objective" possibility of employer to pay larger wages.

The field of empirically oriented research on income justice that applies the factorial survey method is represented by such studies as Jasso, Rossi (1977), Alves, Rossi (1978); Jasso (1978, 1980, 1994, 2007); Jasso, Webster (1999); Shepelak, Alwin (1986) for the case of the USA, Auspurg, Hinz, Liebig (2009); Auspurg et al. (2008); Liebig, Mau (2005a) for Germany, Arts (1985); Hermkens (1986), Hermkens, Boerman (1989) for the Netherlands and Jann (2003) for Switzerland. Some common answer patterns may be observed in these studies regarding formulation of justice judgments. Hence, some important empirical findings may be generalized as universal patterns in justice understanding and evaluation among the citizens of Western democracies. First of all, there is a strong evidence of people taking multiple justice principles into account when ascribing the just earnings to concrete persons with a defined set of personal characteristics. In other words, the considerations of merit and need are persistently apparent in people's judgments in more or less stable proportions. Further, the same combinations of characteristics (conditions) tend to provoke the same reaction of respondents of similar social positions. This means that there is a noticeable degree of consensus with regard to the application of the justice principles among homogenous social groups. Irrespective of nationality, respondents from Western democracies pay more attention to the desert justice principle than to the principle of need when judging the justice of earnings.

Empirical findings generally suggest that the justice evaluations of people with respect to earnings amounts of others depend on who expresses the judgments and who is the object of these judgments.

3.3 International research on distributive justice in post-Soviet states

Cross-national comparative studies provide rich material and fascinating opportunities for testing hypotheses concerning effects of different social structures and cultures on people's justice beliefs. B. Wegener and S. Liebig suggest that it is plausible to assume that the different political and economic "systems" have produced different standards of social justice (Wegener, Liebig 1995: 263). To test this assumption, social scientists addressed the ISJP data, where people from countries with different social systems were asked to answer the same justice-related questions. Indeed, some important differences in attitudes were found. For example, international studies uncovered different perceptions of legitimized income inequality by citizens of the post-communist states and the capitalist West European countries. The post-communist societies have been shown to be more committed to egalitarianism and to show a greater support for a strong role of government in providing welfare (Mason, Kluegel 2000: 15).

The need and equality principles were deeply entwined in socialistic ideology and the level of income inequality in the Soviet Union was assessed as rather low[5]. This fact leads many social scientists to the conjecture that because of the recent socialist experience the need (and equality) principles of distributive justice play greater role at the expense of desert criterion in post-Soviet societies in comparison with the West European democracies. This conjecture provides a basis for the empirical analysis of several studies (e.g., Delhey 2001, Wegener, Lippl, Christoph 2000). However, empirical research has shown that people from post-Soviet states pay as much attention to the information concerning desert when judging the just incomes as do the citizens of West European countries. Based on the data from ISJP 1991, D. Mason and J. Kluegel find "surprising similarities in the attitudes and beliefs on justice issues" in the postcommunist states and West European democracies (Mason, Kluegel 2000: 15). Moreover, G. Marshall et al. (1999), analyzing ISJP data from 13 nations, find that although respondents in the new post-

---

[5] According to Ivaščenko (2010), the Gini coefficient in Ukraine was equal to 23.5 percent in 1989.

communist states of Central and Eastern Europe are more sympathetic to considerations of need than are their counterparts in the capitalist West, it is also true that the principle of reward according to contribution receives widespread popular support in East and West alike. Moreover, some of the scientists argue that the need criterion under certain conditions is taken into consideration in the formerly socialist societies to the same extent as in the Western democracies (Cohn, White, Sanders 2000). One should notice that the datasets used in the studies mentioned here did not include Ukrainian data.

The analysis of the intra-societal differences demonstrates that some general trends established in many Western societies may also be uncovered in the post-Soviet states. For example, there is the self-interest motive that stimulates people who have relatively better positions in a social hierarchy to support the desert principle and to accept larger income inequalities and which stimulates those who are in less advantageous situations to endorse the distribution of wealth according to need and equality principles. In the case of Russia[6], the equity principle is more popular among men, wealthier, better educated and younger people, while the need and equality principles are more supported by women, less educated citizens, older people, and representatives of low-income groups (Aalberg 2003: 60).

The study conducted in post-Soviet Kazakhstan and Kyrgyzstan by A. K. Junisbai (2010) is one of the very rare investigations of the justice attitudes in post-Soviet Central Asia. In his publication of the research findings, the author compares divergent economic trajectories followed by the two countries after the collapse of the Soviet Union and identifies the degree of support for egalitarian principle of distribution among different population groups. The author concludes that the long-term expectations related to individual wellbeing of the citizens in Kazakhstan determine their support of egalitarian principle (the worse the expectations – the larger support). On the other hand, in Kyrgyzstan, such perceived future prospects are irrelevant and superseded by "immediate economic vulnerability." In Kyrgyzstan, the less educated and low-income groups have stronger egalitarian attitudes. With this empirical evidence, the author confirms his hypothesis that according to the underdog principle, the more vulnerable members of the society are more likely to support the egalitarian principle of income distribution (Junisbai 2010: 1683). The data also showed that, in accordance with this principle, the better off urban citizens have less egalitarian attitudes than do the rural population in

---

[6] The data comes from ISJP 1991.

both countries. Another very interesting finding of the study is related to the perception of wealth sources: "respondents in Kazakhstan and Kyrgyzstan identified 'having the right connections' as the most common factor responsible for individual wealth" (Junisbai 2010: 1689). Further, the authors tested an assumption that older people in Kazakhstan and Kyrgyzstan are more likely to be supportive of egalitarian distributive principle than are younger people who came of age after the collapse of the USSR. He conjectured that egalitarian ideology must have shaped the views of people who lived and worked during the years of the Soviet Union. However, the results of empirical analysis revealed the following: "Young and middle-aged people are just as likely to support egalitarian economic justice principles as those who worked most of their life under the Soviet Union and have already retired" Junisbai (2010: 1697). Age of respondents had no significant effect on justice attitudes, so the hypothesis that the Soviet ideology must have shaped the views of the older generations socialized under the conditions of official egalitarianism found no support.

When relying on previous empirical studies of Russian and Ukrainian sociologists, one can distinguish a similar answer patterns among respondents. These patterns point to a rather specific wealth perception in the post-Soviet states. According to empirical results obtained by Russian social scientist T. Zaslavskaya in 1997, people attribute the following issues to the factors of wealth: relationships with powerful people (social networks) (77%), economic system, which allows rich people making profit out of poor (70%), and only after that – talents and skills (41%), opportunity to receive good education and job (40%), luck (28%), and hardworking (21%) (Soroka, Zub 2008). These results suggest that social capital in post-Soviet countries is more important than human capital in securing access to higher social positions and accordingly to higher proportions of common good. In line with these results are the findings of ISJP: S. Stephenson and L. Khakhulina (2000: 96) conclude that the emerging Russian capitalist society at the beginning of the 1990s was not a meritocratic one in terms of actual rewards distribution and state that this society "reproduces in many ways the Soviet features of success. The prevailing model of success in Russia is not so much individual salvation demonstrated through self-denial and hard work … but rather the ability to get access to the systems of social networks."

Empirical evidence from Ukrainian data seems to be a bit controversial with respect to the importance of factors that help people to succeed in life. According to ISSP 2009, 92% of Ukrainians consider having a good education as an important[7] condition to make a career and to attain success, while 88% of respondents attributed importance to the category of "knowing the right people." A slightly lower proportion of the population regards hardworking (85%), having ambition (81%), and coming from a wealthy family (70%) as important factors in achieving success. On the other hand, the data from Omnibus 2009 show that choosing up to 5 most important factors from a list of 13 items[8], people place good education (26%) after "powerful relatives" (51%), "family with high social status" (38%), "rich parents" (37%), "high intellectual capabilities" (30%), "good health" (28%), and "powerful friends" (27%). The apparent inconsistency of the importance of educational attainment could probably be a result of the different question wordings, namely, a stimulus "Ukraine" that appears only in the respective question of the Omnibus 2009. It seems likely that people attribute such a high value to the quality of education in ISSP 2009 because they can generally imagine a successful professional and personal growth among others outside Ukraine. Nevertheless, both studies allow one to conclude that status positions of family members as well as personal social networks play an essential role in shaping the life chances of Ukrainians.

Some scholars stressing the neo-patrimonial character of the Ukrainian society claim that "The marginalization of intelligent and competent people in society and economy is very conspicuous in Ukraine. Ukrainian society is far from being a meritocracy" (Zon 2001: 79). Taking these facts into account, it becomes clear that the real distribution of status positions and wealth in Ukrainian society is defined by a complex set of various factors, among which merit considerations do not always take priority. The answer patterns of Ukrainians suggest that the role of social capital in the society is more important than that of human capital. In situations where distribution of goods is undertaken under constraint of limited resources, people are treated according to their proximity to individuals occupying high status positions rather than according to the desert principle. Such organization of social interactions is typical for countries where the rule of law has not been established yet. Under these conditions, the law generally treats citizens unequally often due to the conniving violation of accepted rules by individuals at the top of the social pyramid.

---

[7] Respondents who marked the answers "essential," "very important" and "fairly important" to the question "Please tick one box for each of these to show how important you think it is for getting ahead in life... how important is having a good education yourself?"

[8] Respondents answered the question "What of the following is important to achieve high social position in Ukraine?"

Based on the Russian data coming from the ISJP, sociologists find that "Support for equal distribution is associated quite strongly with the person's own position in the system of inequalities: lower social class, less education, and perceiving oneself as a loser in the transition process" (Stephenson, Khakhulina 2000: 89). This relationship between economic position and attitudes towards income inequality is generally applicable in any society since it was uncovered in different states and across different time periods.

Jacobs (2006) points to the two prominent tendencies with regard to attitudes towards justice and freedom in the post-socialist countries[9]. On the one hand, people distinctly prefer the orientation towards the desert justice principle and strongly support the idea of equality of opportunity. On the other hand, the majority of the population believes that it is primarily the task of the state to reduce income inequalities in a society.

3.4 Ukrainian and Russian scholars on the distributive justice problem

In this section I briefly review the state of "domestic" research on justice issues. As is commonly the case, the interest to the specific aspects of any social phenomenon inside a country is higher among the scientists of said country. Therefore, one may intuitively expect that an overview of post-Soviet studies on social justice gives an impression of the major focuses, directions as well as major shortcomings and gaps in the state-of-the-art justice research in Ukraine. The international research on justice issues in post-Soviet transition countries was considered separately since the state of social research on the distributive justice in Western Europe and the USA differs starkly from that in the post-Soviet countries. This holds true for many other research areas in the social sciences as well. The difference concerns not only the degree of elaboration of the research problems and consequently the amount of available scientific publications devoted to various aspects of them, but also to an overall focus of justice research and content of the research questions posed in empirical studies.

Post-Soviet sociologists have not that succeeded in elaboration of justice theories or empirical research on different aspects of distributive justice. There are practically no national surveys that could provide the data for applied studies on assessment of just incomes, definition of just tax rates, estimation of social inequalities or preferred principles of wealth

---

[9] Albania, Bulgaria, Czech Republic, Estonia, East Germany, Poland, Hungary, Romania, Russia, Slovak Republic, Slovenia.

distribution. This is not surprising since the post-Soviet states are generally marked by the extremely complicated situation in the social sciences at the end of the 20th and beginning of the 21st century. During the Soviet times, social sciences in Ukraine and other Soviet republics was placed under the pressure of communist ideology. This had dramatic consequences particularly for sociology, which did not exist as an independent social science in the Soviet Union. This circumstance, of course, influenced the path of development of sociology in the affected countries considerably. As a matter of fact, the most experienced sociologists who nowadays constitute the core of sociological community in post-Soviet states, are specialists coming from other disciplines: history, economics, philosophy, psychology, mathematics, etc. Permanent lack of high-quality sociological education and sociological tradition as well as shortage of relevant infrastructure, including access to up-to-date scientific publications at universities and scientific institutes, caused essential difficulties in development of sociological theory and research. Not surprisingly, the recent publications on social justice in Ukrainian and Russian journals for the most part present superficial analyses of certain aspects of this phenomenon, and the empirical studies are often not likely to be methodologically rigorous.

Social surveys in the Soviet Union were extremely rare; therefore, the modern research of transformation suffers in many respects from a problem of the lack of data and empirical analysis ('tabula-rasa-problem' (Delhey 2001: 30). The heritage of 20 years of independent sociological research in Ukraine may be described as rather modest. Still it is worth outlining here in order to depict the challenges for the present work. Since the number of relevant articles and monographs on social and particularly distributive justice published in Ukraine since independence are very rare, I refer in my present overview to the publications of contemporary Russian sociologists as well in order to give an idea of the state of justice research in post-Soviet countries.

In the past two decades, some attempts in Russia and Ukraine to analyze the most well-known western theories of justice (e.g., Gavrilova 2009, Pirogov, Efimov 2008) and to reveal the meaning of the concept through empirical research (e.g., Kirjuchin, Ščerbak 2007, Nazarov 1999) were undertaken. The justice issue is predominantly discussed in the context of political ideologies as a virtue of social system or interpersonal relations. Unfortunately, the majority of the publications present abstract reflections on the issue of justice and offer eclectic, ungrounded speculations on the concept. Such publications produce rather doubtful knowledge, which could neither be applied in theoretical nor in empirical work and poorly (if at all) contributes to the understanding of justice issues. Moreover, there is an overwhelming scarcity of empirical studies on people's justice perceptions, attitudes, and beliefs. The available studies give a reference to justice attitudes' sources and consequences neither on the micro level of human actions, nor on the macro level of social phenomena. A typical feature of many publications devoted to the issue of justice is already habitual inclination of authors towards mosaic overview and often shallow discussions of different conceptions of justice found in philosophical, economic and sociological literature.

Overall weakness of theoretical and methodological background of such studies may be illustrated by many examples[10] that point to a general problem of the underdevelopment of post-Soviet applied social research. This was caused, among others, by scarce access to the relevant up-to-date knowledge in social theories and methods and deficiency in the training of social scientists. Apart from scientific literature published within the frameworks of international projects such as ISJP or ISSP, there are few articles focusing on the problem of people's perception of justice and just inequalities based on national research in post-Soviet states.

In the field of earnings' distribution research in Ukraine, the key focus is placed on description of actual income inequalities (Oksamytna, Khmelko 2007; Doslidžennia 2009; Balakirjeva, Černenko 2009). National surveys show that people have tense aversion against income inequalities that are perceived as very large in Ukraine (Balakirjeva, Černenko 2009: 60). This is not surprising since a very large proportion of the population perceives its place to be in the poor stratum of society. Overall poverty of the population as opposed to elites is a striking characteristic of a modern Ukraine. However, many social scientists point to a shift from absolute poverty towards subjective (relative) poverty of the population during the independence years (e.g., Ivaščenko 2010: 51).

---

[10] For instance, B. Ališev and O. Anikeenok (2007) in trying to define which distributive justice principles are applied by students (sample size = 212) in different situations, confused in their questionnaire concrete principles of distribution such as "to distribute goods equally" with the abstract statement of a kind "to distribute goods in a way that everyone is satisfied." Another example is a paper of O. Komarova (2008), who advocates the idea that "the social justice principle" should be applied in the process of distribution of social transfers, but as with many others, instead of clarifying the idea, she leads the reader astray by providing a number of general ideas and definitions of the notion of social justice taken from diverse sources including textbook of ethics and internet-based collection of students' essays.

A collection of articles edited by R. Ryvkina (2003) combine a number of mostly descriptive but, nevertheless, important studies of social inequalities in Russia. In one such article, O. Kolennikova investigated the just and unjust inequalities in Russia and found that the most striking inequality perceived as unjust was the inequality between higher officials and the rest of the population. At the same time, the most fair inequalities were reported to be those between working people and the unemployed as well as those between highly educated employees and uneducated workers (Ryvkina 2003: 173). These conclusions were drawn from the answer distributions to the relevant survey questions and they point to the overall acceptance of the merit principle among the population. At the same time, perception of the enormous discrepancy between income of high officials and the rest of the population and its active disapproval by respondents demonstrate that the equality justice principle is popular among Russian citizens.

In 2009, Ukraine joined for the first time one of the best-known international comparative studies on inequality and social justice, the ISSP. This survey sought deeper investigation of income inequalities and subjective justice beliefs of citizens in a number of European countries. Appropriate methodology and relatively detailed questionnaire enabled complex analyses of social inequality and income justice from a new comparative perspective. Based on the data from this survey, a number of publications appeared in recent years (e.g., Oksamytna 2010, Ivaščenko 2010, Simončuk 2010, Malyš 2011). The ISSP 2009 data have shown that nearly all of the (95%) Ukrainian population perceives the existing income inequality in Ukraine as unfairly large (Babenko 2009: 12). Some special questions in the ISSP questionnaire concerning perceived actual and just earnings of different occupational groups allowed measuring the perceived unjust earnings inequality in absolute and relative terms. For example, Ukrainians believe that the just earnings of a cabinet minister in the national government should be about two times larger than a salary of a doctor in general practice, while the actual earnings of a cabinet minister is perceived to be 20 times larger than that of a doctor (Ivaščenko 2010: 45). At the same time, the remuneration of one's own labor was predominantly assessed as much less than deserved. In Ukraine, about 80% of people perceive their earnings as unjust, whereas in the developed capitalist democracies, such proportions amount only to 57% on average (Simončuk 2010: 69).

These findings generally suggest that the existing order with respect to income distribution is not considered legitimate by most Ukrainian citizens.

3.5 Measuring justice attitudes in surveys

This section is devoted to the experience of social science in measuring justice attitudes. I briefly discuss the traditional and innovative techniques used in empirical studies on distributive justice and review the instruments applied in large surveys conducted on national and international level with a special focus on Ukraine.

3.5.1 Classic attitudes measuring

There are direct and indirect methods of measuring attitudes in the social sciences. The difference between them is that the first type requires the conscious attention of the respondent and the second does not. The direct measurement of attitudes in surveys has become a standard technique in social science research. Its popularity is associated with higher reliability of data and the fact that it allows for the direct interpretation of results. The two most significant researchers who first developed the direct techniques to measure attitudes in surveys were R. Likert (1932) and L. Thurstone (1928). The Likert scale remains even today the most widespread technique of measuring attitudes in social surveys. The item-based questions in surveys are also prevalent in the field of justice studies.

As a result of rapid globalization, international comparative studies have grown enormously in number and popularity in recent decades. The problem of social inequality and the related issue of social justice perception received their due attention as popular topics that provide important findings for the social stratification theory. Designing the cross-national comparative surveys is associated with multiple challenges and nuances. One of the most complicated tasks is to develop a meaningful questionnaire that can be applied in all participating countries.

Different examples of question wordings measuring justice attitudes may be found in international comparative projects such as International Social Justice Project (ISJP), International Social Survey Programme (ISSP), European Social Survey (ESS), or World Values Survey (WVS). In this paragraph, I provide a number of indicators for measuring different aspects of the justice attitudes from the large-scale cross-national surveys and discuss on their scope of application.

The questionnaire of the ISJP survey comprises questions on sources of poverty and wealth, economic inequality, distributive justice principles, governmental role in distributive processes of a society, personal injustice experiences and subjective social class evaluation. To indicate the level of support for the equality, desert, ascription, and need justice principles this questionnaire employs the following seven items:

1. The fairest way of distributing wealth and income is to give everyone equal shares.
2. It is fair for some people to have more money or wealth, but only if there are equal opportunities.
3. People are entitled to keep what they have earned, even if this means some people will be wealthier than others.
4. People who work hard deserve to earn more than those who do not.
5. People are entitled to pass on their wealth to their children.
6. The most important thing is that people get what they need, even if this means allocating money from those who have earned more than they need.
7. It is just luck that some people are more intelligent or skillful than others, so they do not deserve to earn more money.

Respondents were asked to assess their degree of agreement to each of the statements using a five-term Likert scale: "Strongly agree," "Somewhat agree," "Neither agree nor disagree," "Somewhat disagree," "Strongly disagree." This is the most common method to measure support of the justice principles. Although the statements seem to be easily perceived and understood by respondents, they are highly abstract and this makes it impossible to draw some applied conclusions. For example, answers to the first statement, which deals with the equality principle, neither gives us account on the nature of goods to be distributed, nor on participating subjects. Based on this information, one may assume different answer patterns. This can be illustrated by addressing two extreme cases. For example, it is very likely that people would support equality justice principle to a different degree when they evaluate giving equal shares of cake to all children in a family or giving equal marks to all students irrespective of their knowledge of the subject. Similarly, in this particular question of ISJP relating to wealth and income, there are many options for divergent interpretations. More equal distribution of wealth in a society using the taxation system or equal wages to all employees contrary to market economy mechanisms may imply diverse answers. Therefore, the abstract statements of such kind are to be used with a high degree of caution.

The best-known worldwide survey on social issues – the World Values Survey (WVS) – in which Ukraine participated in 1996 and 2006 asked one explicit question on fairness of income at the individual level. This question was included in the questionnaire in the second wave (2006) and concerned the desert principle of income justice. It described one secretary who worked faster, more efficiently, and more reliably than the other secretary and earned respectively higher income. The question was whether the unequal pay was just. The idea was to test if people believe that the efficiency in the similar work should be rewarded. According to the results, 87.7% of respondents indicated that the additional income for a more productive worker was fair, thus supporting the desert principle.

This evidence was in line with another result from the same survey: on the 10-scores scale, respondents were asked to choose one score between two extreme poles: (1) "Incomes should be made more equal" and (10) "We need larger income differences as incentives for individual effort." For the most part, people tended to choose values closer to the latter statement (the mean value is 6.94, figure 3.1). This outcome points to the overall support of the desert principle among Ukrainians.

Figure 3.1. "How would you place your views on this scale?" In %, WVS 2006, Ukraine

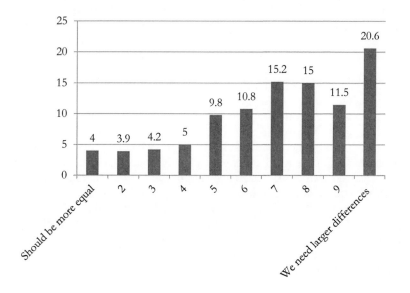

On the other hand, placing equality and desert principles on the same scale may be misleading since it does not help to uncover the support of egalitarian principle in real situations. The results of the European Social Survey (ESS) may serve as an illustration. Expressing agreement or disagreement to the statement "Government should reduce differences in income levels," Ukrainians clearly supported more income equality through governmental actions in the same and following years (figure 3.2).

Figure 3.2. "Government should reduce differences in income levels." In %, ESS 2006, 2008 and 2010, Ukraine

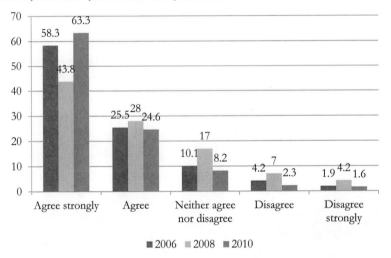

A very popular indicator often used in large-scale surveys concerns the general perception of income inequality by population. It is, as a rule, assumed that if people perceive that the income inequalities are very large, they are more inclined to support policies that equalize earnings. The logic of this assumption is that if people are not willing to smooth the inequalities, they do not perceive them to be large but rather ordinary. An illustration of large support for the equality justice principle may be provided by data from ISSP 2009. According to ISSP 2009, over 95% of the population of Ukraine agreed with the statement, "Differences in income in Ukraine are too large" (figure 3.3) and hence indirectly expressed a wish towards more equal distribution of income.

A general picture may appear extremely controversial. Ukrainian citizens mostly believe that the income differences in Ukraine are too large.

Consequently, they support governmental intrusion in order to reduce income inequality. However, if the question is put differently, they prefer to have larger income differences as an incentive for individual effort instead of supporting more equal incomes. The conclusions concerning support of the justice principles of desert and equality in Ukrainian society drawn from these three answer distributions (figures 3.1, 3.2, 3.3) may be confusing. This issue points to the problem of question wording in surveys that use item-based questions to measure attitudes. The complex nature of justice attitudes comprising different considerations at the same time makes it difficult to distinguish the real meaning of the respondents' answers to such questions. Thus, analyzing the survey data based on similar indicators one should be very cautious when interpreting the results that may, as has been shown, allow for only limited scope of conclusions.

Figure 3.3. Answers of Ukrainian citizens: "Differences in income in Ukraine are too large." In %, ISSP 2009

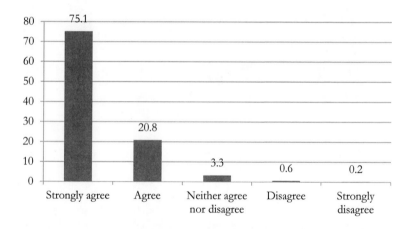

ISSP 2009 used a special block of indicators (table 3.1) concerning actual and just income perceptions. Respondents were asked to provide assessments of actual earnings in different jobs, such as an unskilled worker, a doctor in general practice, a shop assistant, a chairman of a large national corporation, and a cabinet minister in the national government.

Table 3.1. Perceptions of actual and just earnings, ISSP 2009, Ukraine

We would like to know what you think people in these jobs *actually earn*. Please write in how much you think they usually earn each month, after taxes. Many people are not exactly sure about this, but your best guess will be close enough. This may be difficult, but it is very important, so please try.

		Mean (UAH)	Std. Dev.	Median	N
a.	About how much do you think a doctor in general practice earns?	1450.85	602.8	1423.05	1336
b.	How much do you think a chairman of a large national corporation earns?	29279.88	111672.4	10000.00	1003
c.	How much do you think a shop assistant earns?	1274.41	1058.4	1000.00	1475
d.	How much do you think an unskilled worker in a factory earns?	1227.09	1015.8	1000.00	1442
e.	How much do you think a cabinet minister in the national government earns?	39544.72	270776.6	20000.00	1247

Next, what do you think people in these jobs *ought to be paid*? How much do you think they should earn each month, after taxes, regardless of what they actually get…

		Mean (UAH)	Std. Dev.	Median	N
a.	About how much do you think a doctor in general practice should earn?	4277.34	4054.7	3000.00	1581
b.	How much do you think a chairman of a large national company should earn?	14841.26	41702.5	10000.00	1187
c.	How much do you think a shop assistant should earn?	2558.65	2023.2	2000.00	1614
d.	How much do you think an unskilled worker in a factory should earn?	2935.86	3194.6	2000.00	1615
e.	How much do you think a cabinet minister in the national government should earn?	9105.80	11564.9	7000.00	1492

Source: ISSP 2009, author's calculations

This sort of questions enables direct assessment of discrepancies between perceived actual and just amounts of earnings. The ISSP 2009 data for Ukraine (table 3.1) suggest that people generally believe that doctors in Ukraine are severely underpaid (receiving about three times less than they ought to earn), unskilled workers and shop assistants earn about two times less than people think is just, while representatives of economic and political elites such as chairmen of large national corporations and cabinet ministers are highly overpaid. The particularly large standard deviations related to these two latter occupations reflect the low degree of consensus of people concerning actual and just earnings for business and political elites. Together with larger numbers of missing answers to these two items, one may deduce a comparatively low awareness of population concerning actual earnings of these occupational groups. Interestingly, people believe that in the real world, a cabinet minister earns more than a chairman of a large national company, but suggest that it would be fair for representatives of large businesses to earn more than high-ranking state bureaucrats.

3.5.2 Innovative factorial survey design (vignette analysis)

The factorial survey was introduced to social science methods by Peter Rossi (1979), who developed this method in his PhD dissertation on social stratification (Rossi 1951). Since then over last three decades, this method was widely applied in many studies on attitudes and decision-making (Wallander 2009). Social scientists have noticed that in specific research questions, a vignette strategy has many advantages over traditional approach employing item-based type of questions (Beck, Opp 2001, Auspurg, Hinz, Liebig 2009). Factorial survey approach integrates principles of experiment with those of the social survey. The essence of method is that a respondent receives a number of object's descriptions and evaluates them on a specific scale. These descriptions of objects consist of systematically varying characteristics that are deemed to be essential to the respondent's decision. Application of the specific statistical procedures to the data gained by this technique makes it possible to assess the importance of each of the characteristics for the evaluations of respondents.

When applied to the distributive justice studies, the factorial survey approach found a fruitful ground and gained much in popularity. Scholars have underlined that contrary to item-based questions in a survey research, the vignette approach does not ask for the degree of agreement or disagreement with some abstract justice principle, but it translates issues of the reward allocation into situations of real life. As S. Liebig and S. Mau (2005a: 214) note, "The plus side of asking people to evaluate the outcome of a distribution rule rather than the principle itself is that they can combine and mix different justice principles."

Since microjustice is related to the qualifying attributes of individuals (Brickman et al. 1981: 178), the selection of individual characteristics deemed relevant to respondents' justice judgments is the key challenge in a process of developing a factorial survey design. Because every such individual characteristic is associated with a justice principle, the importance of different justice principles to a respondent's judgment may be assessed by analyzing the weight ascribed by respondents to the characteristics used in descriptions of fictitious persons. Table 3.2 summarizes the characteristics treated in different studies in order to measure the importance of major justice principles in justice evaluations of people.

Evaluation of concrete situations using the factorial survey approach provides more refined information on people's justice attitudes inasmuch as respondents in their answers are less affected by the considerations of socially approved behavior. In the case of classic attitude measurement techniques, where respondents express their agreement or disagreement with abstract ideas and principles presented as separate items, people are more likely to reflect the generally accepted norms and describe oneself as acting in accordance with socially desirable standards. Evaluating vignettes implies less influence of social desirability on respondents' answers because of the complexity of depicted situations, which are constructed with an idea that they should roughly resemble real life with its multidimensionality. With this respect, C. S. Alexander and H. J. Becker note that while evaluating vignettes respondents may be less biased because "most people are not particularly insightful about the factors that enter their own judgment-making process" (Alexander, Becker 1978: 95). It is one of the tasks of a researcher to estimate the effects of certain characteristics and their combinations in the vignettes. On the one hand, the vignettes' complexity helps dealing with social desirability effects: respondents are usually not trying to reflect on each justice principle that may underlie every element of the hypothetical description, for example, in order to avoid expressions of discriminating attitudes. On the other hand, complexity of the vignettes (number of dimensions used) and vignette modules in general (number of vignettes per respondent) may affect the answer behavior of respondents if the cognitive load related to handling the task becomes to demanding.

Table 3.2. Operationalization of justice principles in factorial survey studies

Justice principle	Dimensions	Examples of empirical studies
Need	Age	Sauer et al. 2009a, Auspurg et al. 2008, Jasso 2007, Liebig, Mau 2005a, Hermkens, Boerman 1989, Hermkens 1986
	Number of children	Sauer et al. 2009a, Auspurg et al. 2008, Liebig, Mau 2005a, Liebig, Mau 2005b, Hermkens, Boerman 1989, Hermkens 1986, Jasso, Rossi 1977
	Marital status	Sauer et al. 2009a, Liebig, Mau 2005a, Hermkens, Boerman 1989, Hermkens 1986, Jasso, Rossi 1977
	Health status	Auspurg et al. 2008
	Heritage	Liebig, Mau 2005b
Desert	Educational attainment	Sauer et al. 2009a, Auspurg et al. 2008, Jasso 2007, Hermkens, Boerman 1989, Shepelak, Alwin 1986, Hermkens 1986, Jasso, Rossi 1977
	Occupation	Sauer et al. 2009a, Auspurg et al. 2008, Liebig, Mau 2005a, Jasso 2007, Hermkens, Boerman 1989, Shepelak, Alwin 1986, Hermkens 1986, Jasso, Rossi 1977
	Full- or part-time job	Hermkens, Boerman 1989, Hermkens 1986
	Work experience	Auspurg et al. 2008
	Job tenure	Auspurg et al. 2008
	Work performance	Sauer et al. 2009a, Auspurg et al. 2008, Hermkens, Boerman 1989
Ascription	Sex	Sauer et al. 2009a, Auspurg et al. 2008, Jasso 2007, Liebig, Mau 2005a, Hermkens, Boerman 1989, Shepelak, Alwin 1986, Jasso, Rossi 1977
	Ethnicity/race	Shepelak, Alwin 1986
	Economic situation of a firm	Sauer et al. 2009a, Auspurg et al. 2008
	Firm size	Sauer et al. 2009a, Auspurg et al. 2008

Sauer et al. (2011) thoroughly examine the impact of vignettes' complexity on the consistency of respondents' answers, as well as learning and fatigue effects in a methodological study of the application of factorial survey method in general population samples. The authors stress that factorial survey in general is rather demanding in terms of individual cognitive and information-processing abilities of respondents. They use vignettes with five, eight and twelve dimensions and vignette modules consisting of ten, twenty or thirty vignettes per respondent. The results of the analysis of the response time suggests that people need slightly more time for the evaluation of the first few vignettes, after what they learn the rating task and cope with the next vignettes faster. The researchers argue that age and education of respondents generally have no significant effect on the response time and answer consistency, except for very complex conditions (12 vignette dimensions or 30 vignettes). The authors conclude that the factorial surveys are well suited for the general population samples although researchers should not exaggerate with the number of dimensions and vignettes per person. Furthermore, K. Auspurg, T. Hinz and S. Liebig (2009) recommend excluding the implausible (unrealistic) vignettes from the vignette sample, because they affect negatively the general attitude of respondents towards survey and answer consistency of the vignettes evaluated next.

Although a factorial survey applied to relevant research questions assures collection of more valid and precise information as compared to other survey techniques, it is also associated with more time and effort intensive stage of survey design elaboration. While designing a vignette module, researcher's attention should be turned to several important aspects, among them – those related to the efficiency of the vignette sample. Efficiency is understood as "goodness of experimental design" (Kuhfeld, Tobias, Garrat 1994: 545).

The problem of design efficiency arises because "With an increasing number of characteristics considered important from the theoretical point of view and/or with an increasing number of levels distinguished for each characteristic, it rapidly gets impossible for a respondent to judge all vignettes of the complete vignette universe." (Dülmer 2007: 383). A full-factorial design, which consists of all possible combinations of values, and in which "all main effects, two-way interactions, and higher order interactions are estimable and uncorrelated" (Kuhfeld, Tobias, Garrat 1994: 546) may rarely be used in practice. An alternative may be either a random sample from the vignette universe, or a fractional-factorial design. K. Auspurg, M. Abraham and T. Hinz argue that the latter enables to perform reliable hypotheses tests even with a small sample size, contrary to random samples of vignettes, where characteristics and their interactions are more likely to be correlated (Auspurg, Abraham, Hinz 2009: 193).

It means that in order to assure accurate measurement of the effects of each of the dimensions in vignettes, an appropriate ("efficient") vignette sample should be selected and a proper number of vignettes assigned to respondents. At this stage, a researcher is confronted with two questions: how many different vignettes should be selected from the vignette universe and how many vignettes each respondent should evaluate? The answers to these questions define the number of questionnaire versions (vignette decks).

The goodness of the fractional-factorial design is estimated in terms of efficiency. The two criteria of design efficiency are: *balance* (all values appear equally frequently) and *orthogonality* ("variables of different characteristics and all their interaction terms are mutually uncorrelated", Dülmer 2007: 386). A common measure of efficiency often used by researchers is D-efficiency (see Kuhfeld, Tobias, Garrat 1994). As a rule, fractional-factorial designs are considered efficient if the D-Efficieny value exceeds 90.

As discussed above, the number of vignettes per respondent should not be too high, in order to avoid fatigue effects and demotivation to participate in a survey. Multiple factorial survey examples demonstrate that people usually cope well with modules consisting of about 20 vignettes. While carrying out a fieldwork, researchers should assure that the vignette decks are randomly assigned to the respondents. If this requirement is violated, the effects of respondent characteristics may appear to be confounded with the effects of vignette characteristics, which makes estimation of the main effects problematic.

* * *

Each measurement technique is appropriate for studies of a limited range of problems and has its advantages and disadvantages. The choice of a measurement technique depends on research purpose. The prevalent Likert scales are simple in application, imply relatively low costs and are rather well perceived by respondents. These kinds of questions may deliver the information on general perception of income justice in a country, scope of inequalities, support of one or another justice principle in general, etc. However, item-based questions are, as a rule, very abstract. They aim to measure attitudes towards very general justice principles and rather parochial perceptions of general justice-related phenomena. Therefore, application of the item-based questions encounters large difficulties when applied to assessment of relative effect of concrete factors in a set of such factors on the justice judgments of respondents.

If a researcher studies how people's attitudes are affected by different and sometimes controversial considerations (trade-offs of the justice principles), the traditional item-based approach to measurement of attitudes seems to be less suitable. The main reason for this is that even the most detailed and elaborated list of item-based questions may not provide enough of information on people's complex reactions on diverse combinations of circumstances by which the real life situations are marked. Justice attitudes may not be reduced to a simple additive effect of multiple factors since they are also affected by their interactions. This is why an attempt to extract a single factor (e.g., justice principle) artificially from the variety of factors and assess its separate impact on people's attitudes may cause tangible bias in our understanding of people's perceptions. To overcome with this challenge, social scientists have developed an alternative measurement technique based on a quasi-experimental design known in the literature as a factorial survey (vignette analysis). Although the design elaboration of a factorial survey requires considerable efforts, the method enables a more profound and sophisticated examination of many research questions related to people's understanding of social norms, perceptions of diverse life situations and attitudes towards multiple concerns. The potential of this method in the field of empirical justice research will be further unraveled in the next chapters of this book.

CHAPTER FOUR

MIDDLE-RANGE THEORIES AND THE EXPLANATION OF JUSTICE ATTITUDES

What factors may affect the justice attitudes formation? What motives may induce a person to express a particular justice judgment? As noted before, empirical social science research does not deny, but on the contrary even stresses, the dependence of individual attitudes and judgments on personal motives. The justice attitudes are likely to be marked by the considerations of personal interests, internal psychological processes and objective life conditions. In the following sections, I consider basic middle-range theories that describe the socio-economic and psychological mechanisms related to the formation of the justice attitudes. A primary goal of the consideration of these mechanisms is to formulate general propositions concerning the way justice attitudes are formed as well as the reasons for them to remain stable over time or to alter.

4.1 Human capital and labor market theories

As is seen in the analysis of previous empirical literature, the desert justice principle is generally popularly supported. But how can those who deserve higher incomes be identified? What are the criteria of deservingness? One of the possible answers to this question is provided by the human capital theory that was first introduced by G. S. Becker (1964) and became one of the most influential theories in the inequality research. According to his approach, general as well as professional education of employees is positively correlated with their economic productivity. Consequently, it should also be positively associated with their incomes. A better educated person possesses, as a rule, more sophisticated skills. She is able to perform her daily tasks more quickly and to solve emerging problems more efficiently. Further, she is able to cope with tasks that require specific knowledge and may not be accomplished without it.

G. Becker differentiated between general and specific skills of an employee. The first type of skills, according to the human capital theory, enhances productivity in a broad scope of professions and may be applied in different economic sectors and positions. On the other hand, specific skills raise productivity only at specific tasks in a narrower field of use. Employers invest in on-the-job training of their workforce to ensure that they acquire the needed specific skills related to a concrete occupation and crucial to the development and growth of a particular enterprise.

According to the argument of the human capital theory, people who attained better education, either in general, or specific terms, are more deserving because they make a larger contribution to the production of respective services or goods. At the same time, the actual characteristic that is supposed to be directly rewarded is the work performance, not the formal education itself. If the quality of education is appropriate and a person possesses necessary personal characteristics such as good work ethic, accountability and motivation, the link between education and work performance is very strong. On the other hand, if the quality of education is doubtful, or an attained qualification irrelevant, it is not likely to positively affect the work performance of an employee. The relevance of professional qualification is regulated through market mechanisms[1]. According to the market rules, earnings of a labor force unit are defined as an equilibrium point of the demand and supply curves for the respective qualifications on the labor market. The higher the demand for a specific qualification, the higher is the pay employers are ready to give to employees possessing this qualification. On the other hand, the higher the supply of some knowledge or skill, the lower the level of earnings associated with them is.

In terms of justice, it is plausible to assume that people who are guided by the principle of desert would attach significance to such personal characteristics as education, work experience, additional qualifications possessed, profession and occupational position of an employee to judge the just level of income to be earned by a person.

---

[1] This issue is particularly important to keep in mind when dealing with the post-Soviet transition countries because market mechanisms in these countries were first implemented about two decades ago and are still in the process of establishment. Formerly the attainment of specific professional qualifications as well as labor force placement were centrally planned and largely controlled by the state.

4.2 Rational choice theory

Sociologists employ somewhat broader notions of rational choice than it is typically done in economics, where rational choice theory originally stems from. H. Esser argues that the economic rational choice model oversees some important criteria of model building in sociology: for example, the *Homo Economicus* cannot learn and his definition of the situation cannot diverge from the objectively given reality (Esser 1999: 237). If the economic approach postulates that every person maximizes her individual utility based on full information and stable preferences given specific restrictions, sociologists relax many assumptions and suggest that people rather possess beliefs based on incomplete and biased information. Moreover, their preferences may involve altruism, desire to act according to one's values, identity and internalized social norms (Hedström, Ylikoski 2014: 59-60). According to R. Boudon, a "rational-choice-model" can be defined by two features: methodological individualism paradigm and rationality. However, this refers to rationality that includes cognitive as well as axiological reasons (Boudon 1998: 173). P. Hedström and P. Ylikoski (Hedström, Ylikoski 2014) criticize this "wide version" of rational choice theory for providing less theory guidance and constrains. Scholars express doubts whether analytical narratives based on such "soft" theory can produce unique insights about the social world.

Although rational choice theory often cannot account for the full story, in many cases it provides a meaningful explanation of various aspects of human behavior. In the present study, rational choice theory is used not as a general action theory that seeks to be a competing alternative to methodological paradigm of analytical sociology, but rather as a theoretical approach, which stresses the importance of an essential attribute inherent to people in general – striving for the maximization of utility.

Rational choice theory postulates that individual choice of actions is based on the idea that, under certain restrictions, it leads to the best possible satisfaction of preferences (Diekmann et al. 2008). This means that an individual tends to prefer an action that to his or her mind is the best possible option associated with the consequences this person expects. In other words, every person behaves in order to maximize her utility. Nevertheless, the consequences of persons' actions may not always be anticipated in advance and sometimes they are not identical with the desired results.

M. Olson suggests that as far as the economic questions are considered, altruistic behavior is generally regarded as an exception and actions in one's interest are the rule (Olson 1968: 1). Income justice issues are a highly relevant economic question for every individual. Hence, behavior aiming to maximize the share of goods to be received is seen as natural. This idea forms a basis for different justice theories, including the conception of Walster, Walster, Berscheid (1978), which argues that all people attempt to achieve the maximum possible share of goods, and therefore, every person tries to persuade others to accept the distributive rule that is the most advantageous for him: "The most productive worker would try to persuade the others that pay should be allocated in proportion to productivity; the older worker would try to insist that it is only fair that pay should be allocated according to the number of years of service; the poorest worker with no seniority would try to convince the others that since they are all workers together, all pay should be shared equally; and the one with the largest family would insist that the amount of need in terms of the number of mouths to feed should determine the amount of money each worker is entitled to have" (Lerner 1981: 17-18). Similarly, M. Deutsch (1975) assumes that people apply rules of justice as a means to attain their personal goals. He conjectures that the social unit produces its own system of application of the different justice rules since it is the only possible intelligent way to solve the problem. As M. J. Lerner states, "Justice appears to be a rational way for people to coexist and at times to work together as they go about the business of getting what they want for themselves" (Lerner 1981: 20).

In accordance with the rational choice theory, it is logical to expect that people are likely to support the unequal distribution in which they find themselves on the privileged side. As expressed by Frohlich and Oppenheimer (1992: 3ff), "...people are familiar with their own interests, and these interests color their view of what is fair." Accordingly, people with higher education would support higher earnings for better educated groups of the population, while people from deprived regions would seek the redistribution of wealth to secure more than they would receive otherwise. The better off citizens always justify their large incomes by appealing to the desert principle (no matter what makes them think they deserve what they get: a luck, a hard work, personal features or a right to inherit the property of ancestors) and those in worse financial conditions always eagerly support the idea of equality. Those who are at the bottom of income distribution generally appeal more persistently to the egalitarian principle because if their voices are heard, they may expect larger outcomes.

According to the rational choice approach, the support of the equality principle should be apparent among poorer people even in rich societies where satisfaction of simple, basic needs is generally secured for all citizens. In this case, the egalitarian principle is advocated in order to improve one's own relative position in the social hierarchy. As modern sociological and economic literature suggests, the relative position in the social hierarchy is a stronger predictor of an individual's subjective wellbeing (happiness) as compared to the absolute income level (Easterlin 1995, Alpizar, Carlsson, Johansson-Stenman 2005, Clark, Frijters, Shields 2008).

However, in rich welfare societies, the principle of need might have far less importance than in the poor countries, where the majority of population predominantly pursues the goal of survival.

4.3 Socialization and gender wage gap

Social psychologists argue that during socialization, people acquire standard patterns of justification of actual inequalities (Karniol, Miller 1981: 81). This means that individuals learn to accept the existing social and particularly income inequalities as far as they internalize the differentiating criteria such as occupational hierarchy, educational attainment, family status, etc. In this respect, the effect of socialization is strongly intertwined with the effect of the "normative power of the factual." The latest refers to the contribution of actual social mechanisms of wealth distribution in a society to people's acceptance of existing inequalities. Traditionally established social practices that are reproduced in a society for a long time constitute habitual actions that are continually performed without deep reflection every time. This mechanism was expressed in justice theories stating that real social conditions ultimately determine people's attitudes towards "what ought to be" (Homans 1973, Berger et al. 1972). From this point, people tend to tolerate stably existing inequalities as something that is objectively given, and they perceive such inequalities as the natural state of affairs.

The effect of perceived actual inequalities on attitudes toward just income distribution was captured in many empirical studies. The research results have, for example, confirmed that in market societies with more pronounced earnings hierarchies, people tend to accept more income inequality than in more egalitarian state-socialist societies (Kluegel, Mason, Wegener 1995, Gijsberts 2002). Similarly, social scientists have found that formative experiences of different birth cohorts within a society become imprinted in their beliefs and values and make the representatives of such birth cohorts evaluate income inequalities differently (Saar 2008).

One particular case of income inequalities that may be tolerated in a society because of the pervasion of typical social roles cultivated during socialization is gender inequality. It has repeatedly been established in the literature that women usually receive lower earnings as compared to men. Different factors associated with the income penalty for women include segregation of women in low-status occupational positions, their concentration in the low-income economic sectors, interruptions in work history, etc. However, empirical studies show that even after controlling for economic sector, work experience, occupation, education, and other job-related characteristics, gender inequality with respect to earnings is still apparent. Men enjoy higher incomes than women in similar occupational positions with equal productivity (e.g., for post-communist countries Jurajda 2003, Pailhé 2000, Brainerd 2000).

The gender wage gap is a typical social phenomenon for post-Soviet countries (Newell, Reilly 1996, 2001, Pailhé 2000, Brainerd 1998, 2000, Heyns 2005). Although communist ideology promoted the idea of egalitarianism and stimulated the participation of women in the labor market, the origins of the gender wage gap can be traced back to the Soviet times (e.g., Gregory, Kohlhase 1988). Contemporary studies provide evidence that the gender wage gap slightly widened during the transition from a centrally planned to a market economy in many post-Soviet states (e.g., Jurajda 2003, Brainerd 2000, Newell, Reilly 1996).

The scope of gender inequality in earnings is usually measured as a ratio of female to male earnings. Common figures for post-Soviet countries range between 60% and 75%. For example, in 2000, women in Russia received on average 63.3% of men's wages (Ryvkina 2003: 468), whereas in 1989, the mean and median female/male monthly wage ratios in the USSR were 70% and 71% respectively (Atkinson, Micklewright 1992: 97). According to the information provided by the State Statistics Service of Ukraine in 2011 (Dopovid' 2011), the gender pay gap in Ukraine was assessed between 63% and 77% for different economic sectors.

The dynamics of the gender pay gap in Ukraine was extensively studied by I. Ganguli and K. Terell (2005), who used in their analysis empirical data from three different periods: communism (1986), the beginning of transition (1991), and the period when Ukraine started to be considered a market economy (2003). The results show that the gender inequality in Ukraine remains over time: "there is substantial evidence in each year and in each sector that the most important force driving the gender gaps throughout the distribution are differential rewards, or discrimination" (Ganguli, Terell 2005: 4). Scholars state that the gender pay gap is larger in the top deciles of income distribution as well as in the public sector.

Although the gender pay gap in Ukraine is evident, the perception of gender inequality among citizens is rather inconsistent. According to a study of Ukrainian sociologists (Sajenko 2007), only half of the population admits that there exists a gender inequality in Ukraine. Among the Ukrainian people, 62% associate gender inequality in Ukraine with women's rights violation, 6% believes that men are subject to discrimination. Based on a comprehensive attitudes analysis, Ukrainian sociologists conclude that the gender stereotypes are widespread in the modern Ukrainian society. Ukrainians have a clear patriarchal view on gender roles and accordingly define the spheres of main responsibilities of men and women.

As has been established by the social sciences, the understanding of the gender roles develops in the formative period in the process of socialization when people acquire knowledge about central social rules and norms of the society and learn to apply them in specific situations. The process of the adoption of norms consists of two basic components: cognitive and moral (Esser 2001: 371ff, Esser 2000: 69ff). The moral component of the socialization process has a crucial meaning for the study of justice attitudes. Together with adoption of social rules, individuals acquire mental models of the typical situations, frames and scripts of the social behavior. The gender socialization defines the specific norms of socially approved behavior for men and women. Among others, it gives an account on the proportion of paid and household tasks to be ordinarily performed by men and women. In rather traditional societies, such as Ukraine, the gender roles are quite distinct and suppose patriarchal division of tasks: men are expected to care for material wealth of the family and women are expected to assume housekeeping and childcare responsibilities. It should be noted that "it is not only the men who support patriarchal ideas. Many women agree that their full participation in the work-force has had negative consequences for the family, children and themselves, and seem happy to accept the notion that they are the repositories of a set of innate, traditionally feminine personality traits" (Attwood 1990: 212). The success of gender roles' reproduction in a society lies in their wide acceptance by the population among both sexes.

Traditionally, the common socially approved behavior for a woman is to be fully realized as mother and wife and only after that to develop in a professional sense. On the other hand, a male breadwinner whose main task is seen as earning income outside the household is encouraged to advance in the occupational hierarchy and to improve his level of income. The achievements of men in their professional career are criteria of personal success. According to the expectations towards gender role accomplishments, men should especially feel encouraged to place additional effort on the improvement of their income level if they compare their salary with those of their spouses.

Social expectations concerning time use for paid work and housekeeping activities are formed according to priorities of the gender roles. This means that if women in modern Ukraine not only generally perform domestic work but are also engaged in the labor market, their resources of time and effort are split between these two activities. Since these resources are finite, this could be an important argument for the justification of the gender inequality with respect to wages. As it is known, "individuals have multiple social roles and tend to organize their behavior in terms of the structurally defined expectations assigned to each role" (Merton 1967: 170). Therefore, women try to perform both gender and economic roles, however, they almost always prioritize the family.

Psychologists suggest that during socialization, "children apparently learn not only that deviations from equality must be justified but also what types of justifications are culturally accepted as reasonable" (Karniol, Miller 1981: 80). Thus, such reasonable justification for the lower income of women may be based on the idea of the women's priority of family before paid work. Based on the statements of socialization theory, I may conjecture that because of the secondary priority of paid work, women are expected to input less time and effort into it and, therefore, they appear to be less valuable workers and deserve less reward for their work than do men.

According to the status value theory (Berger et al. 1972), every person forms her justice attitudes based on a referential structure. The referential structure consists of beliefs about the actual state of affairs (what is), which is a point of departure for the expectations about the just rewards (what ought to be). Developing this argument, it is clear that in the eyes of a woman her own wages may be justified if she compares her salary to the average salary of her reference group consisting of other women. S. Liebig, C. Sauer and J. Schupp (2011) argue that the cause for not objecting to lower wages might be rooted in the gender-homogeneous occupational environment, where women often have no other opportunity to evaluate their incomes but to compare them with the similar low earnings of other female colleagues. I may assume, though, that because paying smaller wages to women is a common practice in Ukraine, women justify their lower incomes as "usual" and accordingly adjust their expectations.

The reflections presented above lead to a general expectation that the female gender of an employee is associated with a significant negative effect on the amount of income supposed to be just for her.

4.4 Cognitive dissonance and adaptation to reality

Cognitive dissonance theory presented by L. Festinger (1957) suggests that people feel an aversive tension from having two or more beliefs that seem to contradict each other. Discrepancy of beliefs creates a discomfort that people try to reduce by changing their attitudes. The cognitive dissonance may also appear as a result of the inconsistency of reality perceived and beliefs about how it should actually be.

According to E. Walster and G. W. Walster (1975: 23), individuals are motivated to restore justice by applying techniques for either restoration of actual equity or restoration of psychological equity. This means that individuals can reduce their distress stemming from unjust distribution of goods if they distort their perception of reality and persuade themselves that the actual distribution is in fact fair. The crucial role in this process belongs to individual rationalizations. People adapt to an established order by rationalizing and trying to find plausible reasons to justify the actual distribution of wealth. To some degree, this is reflected in a fact that the reality has a shaping effect on people's justice attitudes: "What *is* determines what always *ought* to be. It is this actual, common experience that provides the basis for the general rule of justice" (Homans 1973: 579). This means that justice attitudes are guided by the standards or norms of the actual state of affairs. As mentioned above, the factual has a normative power. This leads to the acceptance of perceived as actual inequalities in income distribution and sometimes it means that people have to color their life conditions to avoid cognitive dissonance.

In order to avoid tension, people naturally perceive their social environment as a given, objective reality that exists according to a certain set of rules, and to operate successfully within this reality, one should take these rules into account. One of the most important elements of the social system – the production and distribution of social goods – is also perceived as an objectively given order. The deficiencies of the distributive system may become apparent after one realizes that the mechanisms of the wealth distribution can be improved. This is often the case when a person is confronted with an example of a deviating situation in which the outcome is more beneficial for its participants. However, the cultural patterns transmitted through the socialization process are, as a rule, deeply imprinted in individual consciousness and may undergo changes on a macro level only in the long term. Therefore, in everyday life situations, people predominantly employ a strategy of adaptation to existent rules, which implies minimum costs for an individual. If it is known that, in a society people, are rewarded according to their educational attainment, it is likely that in order to attain a high level social position in the future, a person will invest in her education. If, on the contrary, institutional framework encourages the application of social networks in order to occupy a higher rung of the social ladder, people are likely to put more effort in the development of their social capital.

* * *

Different mechanisms of the formation of justice attitudes described in this chapter are intertwined in real life and jointly affect the justice judgments of people. For example, the socialization effect may bring into play the mechanisms of the labor market and result in gender income inequalities. This can happen through the selection of men to particular economic branches. According to British psychologist Alison Kelly, the sex difference in school subject preferences is the consequence of the corresponding sex upbringing: "Girls are socialized into having little confidence in themselves; believing the sciences to be more demanding, they are scared to complete" (Attwood 1990: 81). This lack of confidence results in fewer choices of natural sciences as field of studies among female students. As a consequence, a gender distortion on the labor market appears, and the labor supply is limited to a considerably smaller group of the population predominantly represented by male workers. Further, according to the mechanisms of the market, the labor remuneration for the occupations requiring scarce personnel grows.

The adaptation theory and "normative power of the factual" thesis stress the crucial role of the social context for people's attitudes and judgments. Moreover, some general mechanisms may operate differently depending on the social environment. Therefore, it is useful to pay special attention to the analysis of current Ukrainian political and socio-economic development.

Social situations and actors are linked with each other through processes of learning, perception, orientation, socialization, social control, and the "definition of the situation" (Esser 1993: 94). There are objective circumstances (opportunities and restrictions), as well as subjective factors that form the context for individual actions. Specifying the situation in which individuals are embedded, it becomes possible to assess the reasons for their attitudes and beliefs. It is important to take objective circumstances in a particular society into account, while formulating empirically testable hypotheses about formation of justice attitudes. Elaborating hypotheses based exclusively on general theoretical predictions and ignoring the social context of a particular society may sometimes lead to false assumptions. Because some social mechanisms can operate differently depending on a social setting, I am convinced that only after considering the specific situation of a post-Soviet transforming state is it possible to indicate how relevant in this context are those hypotheses derived from the middle-range theories discussed above.

In the next chapter, I highlight the major characteristics of the Ukrainian institutional context and identify the key trends of political, economic and social development of the country. This allows for the determination of some important aspects of distributive mechanisms and typical social practices influencing them in Ukraine. Such basic knowledge is essential to understanding the common response patterns of Ukrainian respondents when answering justice-related questions.

CHAPTER FIVE

UKRAINIAN CONTEXT

In 2004, Ukraine attracted the attention of the international public due to the Orange revolution, which was a peaceful, political mass protest. Since then, the pursuit of European Union integration has been explicitly espoused by the political elite as the development strategy of Ukraine. However, the path to democracy and better quality of life in Ukraine may be depicted as thorny and uneasy, and one of the strongest factors that hinder the rapid transition is the so-called "Soviet legacy" or a path-dependency, which brings considerable social, political and economic challenges.

5.1 Social, economic, and political development of Ukraine after 1991: a brief overview

After Ukraine gained independence in 1991, the state experienced rapid political, economic and social transformations. The transition from a centrally planned to a capitalist economic system was accompanied by democratization processes. Although the population received greater political freedom and free-market opportunities in a relatively short period of time, the rapid changes of the old system had a primarily negative impact on the average Ukrainians' standard of living (Perelli-Harris 2008).

During the 1990s, Ukraine failed to experience a single year of economic growth (figure 5.1). The GDP per capita in this period declined by over 60% (Brück et al. 2010) and the official unemployment rate reached 12%.

Despite all political reforms and economic experiments of new power, the first years of Ukrainian independence did not bring new institutes with legal status and active institutional infrastructure; on the contrary, the social structure of post-Soviet society preserved many status positions for social actors, similar to those they occupied in the past (Golovakha, Panina 2009).

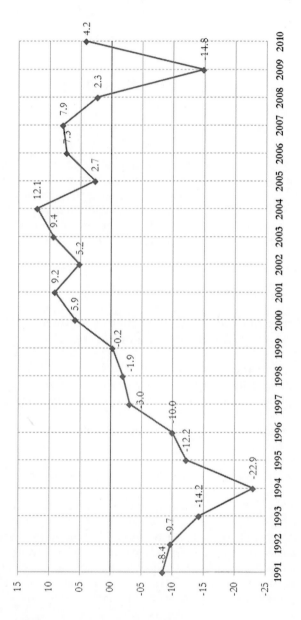

Figure 5.1. GDP growth (annual %), 1991-2010
Source: World Bank (http://data.worldbank.org/)

In 2000-2006 Ukraine's GDP began to grow at an average of some 7.5% a year. The unemployment rate made up 6.7% in 2007 (Human Development Report 2008). This was reflected in the growth of average wages and real incomes of the population. However, 28% of the population still lived below the poverty line (Human Development Report 2008).Ukrainian sociologists Golovakha and Panina (2009) point out the paradox of L. Kučma's ten-year presidency: the economic failure of 1994-1999 was accompanied by political stability while his second presidential term, though economically successful, was characterized by stormy political disturbances. The Orange Revolution in 2004 blocked presidential election and was accompanied by significant rise in optimistic expectations of citizens about the improvement the country's situation (social surveys uncovered a considerable shift in trust in the president, government, political leaders, confidence in the fact that ordinary people can influence political processes in Ukraine, etc.). However one year later, after unsuccessful and partially unreasonable political decisions of the new government and absence of changes in everyday life, the domination of social pessimism in Ukrainian society returned to the previous level. The last years of V. Juščenko's Presidency were marked by the global financial crisis, which affected the Ukrainian economy dramatically: the GDP dropped to -15% in 2009, the official unemployment rose to 8.8% and the country underwent great losses in industrial output. The economic marginalization of households increased substantially during 2009.

Post-Soviet countries have been facing many socio-economic problems during the transition period. Some of them remain unresolved in Ukraine after 20 years of independence: great income inequalities, high poverty rates, the "shadow" economy and informal economic activities, corruption, ineffective tax policy and other. All of these aspects may contribute to the process of shaping the people's judgments on distributive justice; therefore, I suggest going into more detail about some essential characteristics of the modern distributive system in Ukraine.

5.1.1 Income inequality and poverty level

Recent studies provide evidence for increasing income inequalities in Ukraine after the collapse of the Soviet Union (see, for example, Grün, Klasen 2001, Kakwani 1996, 1995). The level of income inequality in the Soviet Ukraine was rather low: the Gini coefficient was equal to 23.5 in 1989 (Ivaščenko 2010). In 1995, the Gini coefficient (based on the disposable income per capita) in Ukraine was assessed as 47.4 (Grün, Klasen 2001), whereas according to the State Statistics Service of Ukraine, it decreased and amounted to 29 in 2008. The income inequality grew enormously after the collapse of the Soviet Union, and it seemed to have smoothed a decade later. However, social scientists argue that some indicators may not be considered reliable because they are based on official statistics that underestimate the amount of income inequality in failing to take into account the "shadow" segment of economy, which, according to expert evaluations, makes up about 30-60% (Balakireva, Černenko 2009, Ivaščenko 2010). Since the "shadow" income is not considered, the Gini coefficient based on official statistics does not give accurate information on income inequality in the case of modern Ukraine.

Recent studies show that income in modern Ukraine is unequally distributed across economic sectors, geographic regions (Balakirjeva, Černenko 2009), and private or state organizations (Gorodnichenko, Sabirianova Peter 2007). Wages in private organizations and enterprises are generally higher than in the state sector: public sector employees in Ukraine receive about 22–32% less in wages than their private sector counterparts (Gorodnichenko, Sabirianova Peter 2007).

The social and income inequalities result from the institutional structure of the post-Soviet Ukraine to a substantial degree. The numerous legal loopholes and the political chaos in 1990s created favorable conditions for the rise of the oligarch class. Many individuals, especially those who had personal connections within the state apparatus, took advantage of the new situation by privatizing enterprises and real estate. Much like Russia, "The main sources of capital of the new elites are money from the Communist Party, privatization of former state property, government subsidies of export-import operations, financial speculation, and criminal activities" (Stepnenson, Khakhulina 2000: 78).

While the new elite was taking shape, the majority of Ukrainian households experienced a period of social and economic marginalization: the hyper-inflation eradicated savings and the real worth of wages and social transfers. Ukrainian society was practically divided into small group of rich and large group of poor citizens for whom the problem of poverty became very acute. The groups most affected by poverty were families with three or more children [1], families with non-working adults and

---

[1] The relationship between poverty and family size was reflected, among others, in very low fertility rates (1.26 in 2009), and as a result, in accelerated population decline. The population of Ukraine decreased from 52 million in 1991 to 46 million in 2009 (Deržavnyj komitet statystyky). The demographic situation is worsened by the external migration and the low duration of life (according to Deržavnyj komitet statystyky in 2009 the average rate for men was 62 years, for women – 73).

pensioners. However, even working citizens were not completely protected from this problem: adjustments of the labor market included wage arrears, forced leave, reduction in hours of work, and in-kind payments (Brück et al. 2010). Extremely low pay was particularly common within the state sector: teaching staff, medical workers and state bureaucrats often received incomes below the subsistence minimum.

People's perception of large social inequality was reflected in many social surveys, in which people strongly advocated implementation of governmental measures to reduce the income inequality. The actual governmental activities concerning redistribution policy through a tax system in Ukraine, however, appear as rather ineffective and dated. In 2004, the Ukrainian government adopted a single tax rate of 15% for personal incomes (Balakireva, Chernenko 2009). Thus, every working person in Ukraine was paying the same 15% tax, and no adjustments of the tax rate were made for people of differing income, number of jobs, family composition, etc.

To assess the incidence of poverty scholars use absolute, relative and subjective criteria of poverty. The absolute indicator of poverty is based on a defined monetary standard that is computed based on some model of consumption. For example, the World Bank defined an absolute poverty line for Ukraine in 2000-2005 as 1813 UAH per person per year (Ukraine: Poverty Update 2007). Using this absolute criterion of poverty, it was uncovered that economic recovery after 2000 led to a rapid decline in the contingent of the population living below poverty line. Figure 5.2 demonstrates that although the absolute poverty in Ukraine was declining, income inequality remained almost unchanged.

The relative criterion of poverty was designed to take into account the level of income inequality in any given society. Relative poverty may be defined as "a lack of income and other resources needed to sustain living standards that are considered normal and suitable within the bounds of a given culture" (Paniotto, Kharchenko 2008: 7).

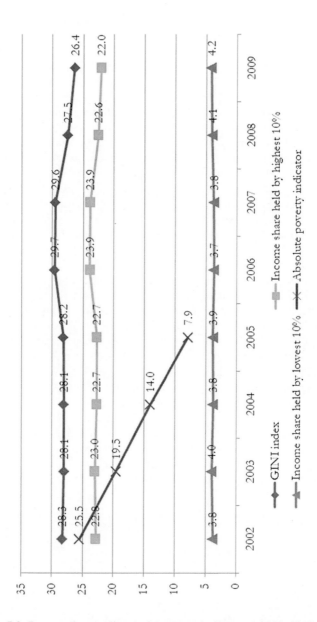

Figure 5.2. Income inequality and poverty indicators 2002-2009
Source: World Bank (http://data.worldbank.org/), Ukraine: Poverty Update 2007.

In the National Human Development Report, the relative poverty line
in Ukraine was "determined as 75 percent of the median level of aggregate
expenditures calculated per one adult. This line was equal to 835 UAH per
capita per month in 2009. In other words, if a household's income
(calculated per one adult) was lower than 835 UAH, this household was
considered economically excluded on the basis of income level. Thus, in
2009, 26.4 percent of households were considered as excluded." (UNDP
2011: 56). Using the same computation strategy, V. Paniotto and N.
Kharchenko (2008) demonstrate that the relative poverty in Ukraine was
rather stable from 2000 to 2006[2].

Table 5.1. Subjective poverty perception in Ukraine, 1994-2010

"Please, assess the standard of living of your household"									
	1994	1996	1998	2000	2002	2004	2005	2006	2008	2010
The highest	0.3	0.1	0.1	0.2	0.1	0	0.4	0.3	0.1	0
9	0.1	0.1	0	0.1	0	0.1	0.1	0.2	0.1	0.3
8	0.2	0.4	0.3	0.2	0.1	0.3	1.1	0.8	1.3	1.3
7	1.4	0.7	0.8	1.7	0.9	0.9	1.9	2.7	3.9	2.8
6	3.3	1.8	1.8	1.8	3.7	5.3	4.6	5.3	5.1	5.7
5	13.4	10.2	9.1	11.2	21.8	22.6	18.6	19.7	22.8	19.3
4	16.3	12.6	11.4	13.8	26.5	29.2	19.6	20	21.7	19.9
3	27.9	25.5	26.6	26.6	22.6	20.7	30.1	30.6	26.1	27.4
2	17.6	18.2	19.3	19.8	17.8	15	12.3	11.7	11.3	14.1
1	8.2	12.6	14.8	12.4	3.2	3.3	6.6	4.9	4.3	5.3
The lowest	11.3	17.6	15.7	12.2	2.4	2	4	3.4	2.7	3.6

Source: Vorona, Šulha (2010).

The subjective criterion of poverty reflects people's perceptions of
their economic situation. As a rule, it is assessed through social survey
data, for example by using such questions as "Please, assess the standard
of living of your household" (table 5.1) or "Please assess the level of well-
being of your household in general over the last 2-3 months" (Vorona,
Šulha 2010). The latter defines the insufficient income to secure needed
foodstuffs as an indicator of poverty. This measure was shown to
correspond with the absolute poverty indicator (Paniotto, Kharchenko

---

[2] The values range from 26.4% in 2000 and 28.1% in 2006 (Paniotto, Kharchenko
2008: 7).

2008). Alternatively, other approaches may be employed to assess the incidence of poverty in Ukraine. For instance, Omnibus 2009 asked respondents to compare their monthly income per capita with the living wage indicated in the questionnaire. According to the data, about 21% of the population stated that the average income per capita in their household was less than the living wage[3].

Rural populations are more strongly affected by poverty as compared to dwellers of large urban centers, and the gap in living standards continues to widen (Vlasenko 2008, Cheren'ko 2008). In line with the literature on poverty, greater poverty risks are realized among households with children and less education (Brück et al. 2010).

5.1.2 Official and unofficial income, corruption and the shadow economy

In post-Soviet countries, there was no tradition of formal institutional rules that constrained the state from acting arbitrarily. This was reflected in the insecurity of human rights and unreliable scope and enforceability of laws. Under these conditions, "interpersonal trust seems to be more important in facilitating economic activity where formal substitutes are unavailable" (Knack, Keefer 1997: 1284). This, among others, explains the prevalence of shadow economy as a form of informal relations.

Shadow economy concerns tax evasion during diverse financial operations including remuneration of labor. One of the most popular forms of shadow income that might distort the official view of income distribution is the so-called *"salary in envelope"* – a wage or a part of a wage in cash given to an employee without being appropriately registered by the accounts department of the institution. The entire amount of earnings paid to an employee in the form of informal payments is typical for informal employment, which is not based on a written contract but rather on an oral agreement between employer and employee. On the other hand, partly informal wages are seen as an important additional share of income necessary to correct for the generally low level of official incomes in Ukraine. Informal arrangements make employees extremely vulnerable and dependent on the decisions of employers, who under such conditions have a very high discretionary power. S. Barsukova (2003: 395), studying the sector of informal employment in Russia, states that even those

---

[3] The living wage made up 607 UAH in 2009 when the Omnibus 2009 survey was conducted. One should notice, however, that this figure underestimates the true cost of everyday life in Ukraine.

persons who have signed employment contracts are often involved in informal interactions since official contracts do not always determine the actual conditions of employment. Employees are often warned beforehand that the actual earnings and other working conditions may diverge from those stated in official agreements.

According to Balakireva and Černenko (2009) 21% of respondents representing the economically active population in 2009 gave a positive answer to the question: "Do you receive your wage or a part of your wage unofficially, by passing the accounts department, as one says 'cash in hand', 'in envelope'?," while 7% of respondents refused to answer this question. There is good reason to suspect that the prevalence of shadow salaries is underestimated through social surveys because respondents are usually not willing to share this kind of information.

Informal economic activities exist outside the formal state regulation and are deeply entwined in Ukrainian everyday life in different forms, including household subsistence activities and illegal trading (Wallace, Latcheva 2006). Unofficial wage is only one type of informal economic behavior, which generally was an essential part of the former communist economies[4] and remains now an important part of the transition economy of Ukraine. According to the study of Schneider (2002), the size of the informal economy in 2000 amounted to 52.2% of GDP.

Another widespread phenomenon related to the informal economic behavior and typical for post-communist developing states is corruption. A Transparency International survey in 2009 showed that Ukraine was one of the most corrupted states among CIS countries[5]. Although corruption is often seen as operating at the high political or business level, the biggest issue for the majority of households is a widespread phenomenon of "everyday corruption." This type of corruption is represented by informal payments for access to services or goods to which people are normally entitled (e.g., to get an appropriate medical care, to obtain entry to university, to register a dacha, etc.). A. Polese (2010), studying illegal transactions in Ukraine, finds that people are inclined to criticize the corruption on the governmental level, but they often regard some payments, especially to medical workers or teachers, as a kind of "gift" and expression of gratitude, without which representatives of these professional groups would not survive. According to recent studies in

---

[4] Golovakha and Panina (2009) name the following Soviet "shadow" institutes: shadow production and profiteering from commodity deficiency, protection and corruption, organized crime, double moral standards for the public and private moral positions.

[5] http://archive.transparency.org/policy_research/surveys_indices/cpi/2009/cpi_2009_table.

Ukraine, teaching staff, medical workers and policemen belong to the three most corrupted professions in this sense (Stan korupciji 2007: 18). Round and Williams (2010) argue that the strategies of employers to pay low wages and/or pay cash in hand mean that employees have little choice but to use informal tactics to negotiate these processes.

The informal economic behavior is facilitated by the social networks that are extremely important in Ukraine, first of all because of their crucial role in coping with economic difficulties (Round, Williams 2010). Hence, the popularity of informal economic activities may be seen as a reaction of the population to the unstable and difficult socio-economic situation in the country. Very often official wages in Ukraine do not suffice to support family, and, as a result, people are forced to pursue their basic economic survival through other means.

There are many reasons for the flourishing sector of informal labor relations in the post-Soviet states including shortcomings of labor and tax legislation, discrepancies between legislation and culturally determined tradition of relationships between employer and employees, and weakness of trade-unions and other civil society organizations[6] (Barsukova 2003: 400ff). The rule of law has not yet been established in Ukraine, and, as a natural consequence of that, Ukrainian society is a low-trust society with underdeveloped horizontal cooperation networks (Zon 2001: 77). The lack of accountability in many formal agreements and procedures generally precludes the development of market economy in Ukraine.

5.1.3 Educational system and labor market

The educational system and labor market were strongly affected by the transformation processes. The formerly planned Soviet economy was based on the idea of state ownership of the work force. The state was responsible for the training of the workforce and bore all educational costs. Labor was allocated by the centrally planned system to the priority sectors of the economy and wages were assigned according to a tariff wage grid for each job category. As a result, the relationship between effort and wage became weak. According to Katz (2001), wage premiums for the highly educated workforce were eroded by the pay differentials in favor of manual workers with low educational attainment. Because of the political priority for the development of heavy industry "the earnings of highly educated specialists in a tertiary sector fell far below those of industrial

---

[6] For more on the weakness of civil society organizations in Ukraine, see Gatskova, Gatskov (2012).

workers" (Pohorila, Slomczynski 2000: 57). Returns to schooling under planning were low, and this resulted in the low efficiency of human capital utilization. However, recent empirical studies reveal that returns to education tended to rise after the market reforms took place (for example Fleisher et al. 2005, Arabsheibani 2007). On the one hand, the level of education strengthened the influence on the personal wages in Ukraine; on the other hand, the quality of education during the transition suffered from funding cuts, lower teacher salaries, textbook shortages and poor maintenance of facilities (Perelli-Harris 2008). This negatively influenced the general quality of education in the country and led to the sinking value of formal educational attainment.

Transformation processes have altered the transition from school to work and the task of entering a stable job after completing education was practically removed from the state's responsibilities. New risks and opportunities appeared for young people in Ukraine. Because of rapid changes, some of the former qualifications became obsolete and required adjustment to the demands of the new system. Unfortunately, the effort of government was not enough to ensure the correspondence between the expectations of employers and the output of the educational system.

M. Gebel and I. Kogan (2011) investigate the school to work transition and early career processes in Ukraine during the transformation based on the data from the representative large-scale survey "Youth Transition Survey in Ukraine 2007." The researchers come to the conclusion that although some scientists (e.g., Round, Williams, Rodgers 2008) argue that access to employment is provided exclusively through personal social networks, there is convincing evidence that higher education opens the way to high-status and stable employment among young labor market entrants in Ukraine (Gebel, Kogan 2011: 293). They find that students who study part-time or by correspondence quickly enter the labor market as a rule. The authors point to the prevalence of a firm-based training in Ukraine conducted on the job after leaving the educational system contrary to a practical training integrated into initial education. Since work experience is required for the overwhelming part of vacancies, it became common to receive first work experience during the last two-three years of higher education. This increases the chances of entering the labor market more quickly and on better terms.

In Russia[7], about 75% of employees, irrespective of whether they are employed officially or informally, state that representatives of their

---

[7] Since no literature was available for Ukraine, I refer to the empirical evidence from Russia. The tendencies in both post-Soviet countries have much in common and therefore studies in one country may illustrate the same processes in the other.

occupations mostly enter the labor market through personal social networks (Barsukova 2003: 395). In line with this study, V. Yakubovich (2005) finds that personal ties play a very important role in finding jobs in the post-Soviet Russia and states that the 1990s are generally characterized by weak labor legislation and low priority given to meritocratic principles and practices that allow employers to disregard official labor market regulations and practice arbitrary hiring.

5.1.4 Regional disparities

Administratively, Ukraine is divided into 26 units including 24 oblasts, the capital city Kyiv and the autonomous republic of Crimea. Based on historical development of the country, modern literature traditionally distinguishes four regions: East, West, Center and South[8] (table 5.2). Sometimes a more rough distinction of two regions instead of four is made: "Generally, analysts draw a line along the Dniepr river, dividing the country into a Russified and heavily industrialised East, and a more ethnically Ukrainian, Western-oriented West" (Kubicek 2000: 273).

A powerful contemporary socio-political discourse points to pronounced economic, political and cultural differences between Ukrainian regions: "The effects of divergent historical experiences, of differential exposure to the world outside the former Soviet Union, and of divergent industrial structure – all point in the direction of enormous attitudinal and evaluative cleavages across the regions of Ukraine." (Zimmerman 1998: 43).

Table 5.2. Four regions of Ukraine and oblasts constituting them

West	Center	South	East
Volyns'ka	Vinnyc'ka	Dnipropetrovs'ka	Donec'ka
Zakarpats'ka	Žytomyrs'ka	Zaporiz'ka	Luhans'ka
Ivano-Frankivs'ka	Kyjivs'ka	AR Crimea	Kharkivs'ka
Lvivs'ka	Kyiv	Mykolajivs'ka	
Rivnens'ka	Kyrovohrads'ka	Odes'ka	
Ternopils'ka	Poltavs'ka	Khersons'ka	
Khmel'nyc'ka	Sums'ka		
Černivec'ka	Čerkas'ka		
	Černihivs'ka		

---

[8] The attribution of oblasts to the four regions of Ukraine may differ in the literature. I use in my study the approach of the IS NASU.

The strong regional divide was unveiled during the Orange Revolution of 2004-2005, when the voting behavior of people suggested two distinct patterns. The majority of the population in the West supported the "orange" opposition, while inhabitants of the Eastern region voted mostly for a more conservative Russian-oriented candidate (Katchanovski 2006). R. S. Clem and P. R. Craumer (2008), in their study of voter preferences for parties and voter turnout across the regions of Ukraine, conclude that a relatively stable electoral landscape had emerged by the time of the parliamentary elections of 2006 and 2007 and point to an established divide between nationalist West and the Russian-oriented East and South. This and other studies have shown that geographic proximity to the bordering states – Russia in the East and European Union in the West – has an impact on the attitudes and orientations of people in the respective regions of Ukraine. Over the past two decades, national social surveys have repeatedly captured substantial disparities in attitudes and characteristics of dwellers of the Eastern and Western regions concerning wide range of social, political, economic, language, religious and other issues (table 5.3).

Table 5.3. Characteristics and attitudes of citizens by region

	West	Center	South	East	Total
What language do you usually speak at home? N=1794, %					
Mostly Ukrainian	92.8	61.1	17.2	6.1	44.1
Mostly Russian	1.5	22.1	56.2	76.8	38.9
Ukrainian and Russian	4.9	15.6	25.1	17.2	16.2
Other	0.8	1.1	1.5	0.0	0.9
Your nationality? N=1789, %					
Ukrainian	98.7	92.6	67.0	64.8	80.9
Russian	1.0	6.9	29.4	34.2	17.7
Other	0.3	0.6	3.6	1.0	1.4
How do you regard the idea of Ukraine's joining the union of Russia and Belarus? N=1792, %					
Rather negatively	45.4	24.7	10.8	4.0	20.9
Hard to say	29.5	26.8	12.9	9.8	19.9
Rather positively	25.1	48.5	76.4	86.2	59.3
How do you regard the idea of Ukraine's joining the European Union? N=1791, %					
Rather negatively	9.3	13.2	26.6	35.4	20.9
Hard to say	38.1	33.3	41.1	42.2	38.4
Rather positively	52.6	53.5	32.4	22.4	40.7

Source: Omnibus 2009, author's calculations.

Scholars mostly ascribe the origin of economic, cultural and ethno-linguistic regional differences to historical experiences. V. Mykhnenko (2010: 141) studies the divergent economic development of Ukrainian oblasts and argues that "the Ukrainian space-economy is best understood as a series of historically rooted and relatively geographically bounded regional economies that are increasingly functionally integrated yet externally oriented."

Recent results of the studies in the social sciences have demonstrated a substantial explanatory power of regional differences. This led to the growing importance of the incorporation of regional perspectives into the analysis of empirical data on different issues ranging from aggregate economic efficiency analysis (Demchuk, Zelenyuk 2009) and assessment of hospital efficiency (Pilyavsky et al. 2006) to research on national identity (Shulman 2006) and descriptions of demographic processes at the regional level (Murphy et al. 2013, Rowland 2004).

Many scholars recognize the importance of regional division for the analysis of people's attitudes and provide evidence for the position that regions not simply be reduced to compositional effects. For example, regional division in Ukraine was shown to be one of the key determinants of political attitudes even under the consideration of ethnical and linguistic characteristics of citizens (Barrington 2002, Barrington, Faranda 2009). In the Western region, where more agricultural and rural oblasts are located, the poverty rate is higher than in the more industrially developed Eastern regions (World Bank 2005).

5.2 Socialism and capitalism

Scholars argue that the need and equality justice principles were deeply entwined in socialist ideology. R. Ryvkina (2003: 59ff.) describes the process of egalitarian principle inculcation in the mass consciousness of Soviet citizens during the socialist period of 1917-1991 and emphasizes that the goal proclaimed by the ruling communist party was to create a classless society, which implied overcoming three types of social inequalities: first, between urban and rural areas; second, between intellectual and manual workers; third, among different social classes, such as intellectuals, working class and peasantry. According to the socialist ideology, the vast party apparatus had to direct its primary effort to promote the idea of equality and its priority over social inequalities through all available channels: mass media, schooling institutions, etc.

The idea of equality was among other implemented as a one-size-fits-all approach (*uravnilovka*), which provoked negative reaction from the intelligentsia. The principle of, "each according to his ability; to each according to his needs," introduced by K. Marx and later developed by V. Lenin, was also important part of ideological doctrine of communism. This justice principle, however, remained to be a statement of utopian character unrealized in the Soviet Union. Nevertheless, ideological upbringing considerably affected personality formation of several generations of Soviet citizens.

5.2.1 *Homo Sovieticus*

No matter how successful some political or economic reforms may be, 20 years of post-Soviet transformation was too short of a period to extinguish completely the "Soviet mentality" and the Soviet relationship between the state and the individual.

The features of the "Soviet personality" were comprehensively studied by Juri Levada, who analyzed the attitudes, beliefs, and values of people in Russia in the context of (post-)Soviet social institutions and portrayed a socio-cultural type of personality that he introduced into the social sciences under the notion of *Homo Sovieticus* (A. Golov, Ju. Levada 1993). According to Levada's description, *Homo Sovieticus* is a "man of the crowd," a "deindividualized" person who seeks to be no different than others in any respect. Such a person has a paternalistic view of the state and may be controlled by it easily. The *Homo Sovieticus* sociocultural identity was intensively formed in the process of socialization in a large, all-encompassing network of state institutions and structures[9]. Individual initiatives that did not fit into the framework of Soviet state institutions and ideology were suppressed.

Ideological socialization and institutional mechanisms were directed towards formation of a deep belief in the state's patriarchal role in the life of each citizen of the Soviet Union. Russian sociologists L. Gudkov, B. Dubin and N. Zorkaya (2008), studying the potential for development of civil society in modern Russia, describe the relationship between *Homo Sovieticus* and the state as asymmetric. On the one hand, the state has a

---

[9] The official community life in the Soviet Union started for the 7-year old children in the *oktiabriata* organization established by the state in schools. As a rule, children were divided into 5-member groups called "stars" – a five-pointed star was one of the symbols of the Soviet Union. The major task of *oktiabriata* organization was to prepare children to become a member of the *pioneer* community. An appropriate ideological socialization was continued for young adults in the *komsomol* organization and for the most successful young people in the communist party.

great power and a leading role in the organization of the individual's life; a person is fully oriented on state forms of social control and reward. On the other hand, *Homo Sovieticus* knows that the state will undoubtedly trick and try to give to a person less than he is supposed to be given, that it will exploit a worker and give him only the minimum of means for survival. That is why *Homo Sovieticus* tries by all means to avoid responsibilities and obligations: he or she may do work carelessly, pilfer, etc. These personality features were naturally cultivated under the centrally planned system.

Some scientists argue that specific features of the system of values, norms and behavioral patterns typical for post-Soviet states may be traced back not only to the communist but as far back as the Tsarist past. H. van Zon (2001) suggests that it is marked by three major characteristics when describing the post-Soviet psychological syndrome: the cult of power, the cult of dependence and the marginalization of intellect. The author argues that the totalitarian rule of the communist party created a cult of power in a system, where everyone was subordinated to a central power: "Because of the long history of absolutist power and the way power is exercised, people have generally become very compliant and accept almost everything that is imposed on them" (Zon 2001: 77). The cult of power has led to a culture of dependence, which is reflected in reluctance to take the initiative and to participate in community life actively. As a result, there is an overwhelming popular perception that the (economic, political, environmental, etc.) situation cannot be changed. Acting or thinking independently was always punished. This led to a marginalization of intelligent people and a tangible lack of analytical strategic thinking among ruling elites.

As new democratic institutions and capitalist market economy began to replace the dictatorial communist regime and planned economy in Ukraine, the country knew no previous tradition of these fundamentally different forms of social, political and economic organization. Even though a new institutional environment seemed to appear in Ukraine after collapse of the Soviet Union, the majority of bureaucratic positions were still occupied by the same people as before. The interaction mechanisms previously existing between these positions preserved and those occupying them were naturally acting in many respects in the same way as before.

Under the conditions of a high uncertainty in the public sphere during the transition period, the civil society in Ukraine was rather weak, and a specific paternalistic character of linkage between the state and individual was constantly reproduced. The state was the only employer and, at the same time, the only guarantor of social security in the Soviet Union. This image is likely to have remained in the mass consciousness of people, and it is reflected, among others, in their perceptions of the state as a powerful supra-individual body, independent of people's actions and views, that is the only responsible actor for the current situation in the country. The expectations of Ukrainians towards the state are deeply grounded in the perception of the state's obligations concerning social security and provision of acceptable quality of life through mechanisms to which the population was already accustomed (among others, the adequate labor remuneration).

The formative influence of the ideological socialization in the Soviet Union had large consequences for the social interactions in the post-Soviet Ukraine. Since the idea of democracy is based on the principle of individual participation, the mentality of *Homo Sovieticus* was incompatible with the democratic choice of society. The case of post-Soviet countries demonstrated that democratic institutions (e.g., parliament, elections) may formally exist despite deficiencies in essential democratic mechanisms. In order to address these inconsistencies political scientists often refer to the concept of political culture.

5.2.2 Political culture of Ukraine

The concept of political culture was introduced into the social sciences to account for the subjective level in political analysis, a phenomenon often overseen in the analysis of objective structures of political institutions. The political culture approach was developed by G. Almond and S. Verba (1963) in their famous study on political orientations of citizens and their relation to the stability of political system. Researchers focused on the consistency between structure and culture and found that this consistency is a factor of political stability. The results of G. Almond and S. Verba demonstrated that the implementation of democratic institutes does not guarantee stable democracy. Authoritarian systems may also become stable if the political system and orientations of citizens are consistent, as sometimes the simple prevalence of people's apathy suffices for it.

The scholars defined three ideal types of political culture: parochial, subject and participant. The parochial political culture is characterized by the absence of political knowledge and ambiguous feelings towards political system among people. In such a society, political actors often have diffused roles that combine political, economic and religious aspects. In the subject political culture, people have cognitive, affective and evaluative attitudes towards the political system. However, they are mostly output-oriented and do not consider themselves as active participants of political life. In contrast to that, the participant political culture originates when citizens possess comprehensive political orientations and actively contribute to political life.

The political culture approach considers three components of people's orientations: cognitive, affective and evaluative. These components relate respectively to knowledge about political situation, emotional support or rejection of it and formulation of judgments concerning political processes and elements of political system.

The Tsarist Empire and Soviet heritage contributed considerably to the formation of the patriarchal orientations of Ukrainian population. The results of social surveys in 2010 indicated that about 64% of Ukrainian citizens expressed patriarchal political orientations by agreeing with the statement "A couple of strong leaders can do more for our country than all laws and discussions." A very large part of the adult population (50.7%) was unable to identify a political ideology with which they affiliated and about 84% did not belong to any civil society organization, including political, professional, ecological, sports, leisure and religious associations (Vorona, Šulha 2010). These results point to some typical characteristics of the parochial and subject political cultures: answer patterns of people uncover the prevalence of patriarchal views, output-orientations and the missing perception of the own active role in a political process.

The conception of political culture is very important for studying transforming societies because it helps to understand scientifically a national "mentality" that is so often appealed to in the public discourse when discussing the numerous failures of independent states and the inconsistency of attitudes and beliefs captured in social surveys. The conception of political culture considers the elements of national history and characteristics of modernity and provides a reasonable explanation of the ostensible ambivalence in attitudes of Ukrainians.

5.3 Situational mechanisms: concluding remarks

This section presents the hypotheses drawn from the statements of the middle-range theories and the background information on the transformation process and its consequences in Ukraine. In order to explore the complexity of justice attitudes in this study, I rely on the general theoretical framework of the multiprinciple justice theory, which recognizes the multidimensional nature of justice and considers three basic justice principles: the principles of desert, equality and need.

Three types of hypotheses are formulated below. The first type concerns the effect of application of the three basic justice principles by people while judging the just incomes in general. The second type of hypotheses deals with situations where different justice principles are applied in concert and therefore the effect of interacting justice considerations is more complex. Finally, as considerations of different kinds may affect the judgments of people of different socio-demographic profiles, the effects of these characteristics on the justice judgments of people must be studied as well. In other words, the third type of assumptions deals with the divergent application of justice principles across different population groups.

From the perspective of human capital and market theories, people guided by the desert justice principle would ascribe *higher incomes to persons possessing better education, having higher work performance and occupying higher positions in the occupational hierarchy.*

Better education is supposed to be rewarded to the extent to which it contributes to the development of professional qualifications and skills of employees in both general and specific terms. Human capital theory generally regards income differentials as returns to investments into education and professional training (Becker 1964, Mincer 1974, Abraham, Hinz 2005). At the same time, this relationship is likely to be distorted by the transformational processes in this context. As noted above, the system of education in Ukraine was negatively affected by the transformation. As a result of reforms in the educational system, decreasing wages of the educational/academic staff and negative trends with respect to corruption practices, formal educational attainment in modern Ukraine does not necessarily reflect the level of skills and competences of its holder. Under conditions of widespread corruption practices in educational institutions, the official diplomas and grades may indicate different levels of knowledge and skills in different cases. For example, the diploma of a higher education may equally be held by a person who successfully acquired some specific qualification as well as a person who simply "bought" it. In the latter case, a diploma is obtained as a result of an informal payment and has nothing to do with an investment in human capital. It means that corruption in educational system "undermines quality and credentials of academic degrees" (Osipian 2009), and this could affect the judgments of respondents, assessing the desert of persons with different educational attainment. Moreover, recent research has demonstrated that in Ukraine, a higher value is often ascribed to on-the-job training of employees than to schooling in the educational institutions. These reflections lead to an assumption that *the theoretically suggested positive effect of educational attainment on just amount of income in judgments of Ukrainian citizens will be muted or even become insignificant.*

Another important desert-related characteristic is one's occupational position. In a meritocratic society, a system of social institutions is organized in such a way that more talented, skilled, qualified and better-trained individuals occupy higher positions in the occupational hierarchy. People are selected in occupations in correspondence with competences required to fulfill the respective tasks most effectively. Better-trained and skilled individuals are more effective in fulfilling complex tasks and can often cope with the broader scope of responsibilities. Therefore, societies try to reward those at the top of the occupational hierarchy by providing higher earnings for their work. The earnings should be large enough to cover the requisite educational expenses and should be in line with one's effort and professionalism. These better paid occupations are generally more prestigious: "The prestige position of an occupation is apparently a characteristic generated by the way in which the occupation is articulated into the division of labor, by the amount of power and influence implied in the activities of the occupation, by the characteristics of incumbents and by the amount of resources which society places at the disposal of incumbents" (Hodge, Siegel, Rossi 1964: 287). Hence, I expect *the prestige of professions to be positively associated with the earnings perceived as just in Ukraine.* However, due to the political priorities of the Soviet state, the prestige of jobs occupied by manual workers was artificially maintained at a much higher level than might be expected from human capital theory. This was achieved through different mechanisms including ideological propaganda and the system of pay grids. The Soviet past may have affected the perceptions of the population in the modern Ukraine. Moreover, scholars argue that the today's Ukrainian society is far from being meritocratic because of the incidence of informal sector. Job positions are often filled through personal connections rather than fair selection procedures, and the wages often consist of official and unofficial part (cash-in-hand). From this point, *the assessment of official just wages by occupation in a transformational society may not appear to correspond to the prestige of these occupations as they might in a country with an established tradition of the rule of law.*

Against this background, the direct indication of work performance appears to be the most appropriate measure of personal merit. I hypothesize that *the positive effect of work performance on perceived just earnings will be strongest among other desert-related characteristics.*

Natural individual characteristics such as age, sex, nationality, race and others have, on the contrary, nothing to do with the merit of an individual. Therefore, if they appear to be significant to people's justice judgments, then they indicate inequalities perceived to be just by the population. If, on the other hand, the equality principle is applied to the assessments of just incomes, these natural characteristics should not have a significant effect.

One may argue, however, that the age dimension can represent the need of an individual as well: it is known that the average costs for the healthcare grow as one ages. On the other hand, age can reflect one's merit, since it is strongly correlated with one's work experience and level of professional qualification. In the specific context of Ukrainian post-Soviet reality, the meaning of large work experience can nevertheless mean quite the reverse. A young independent state under the newly arising market conditions and large social transformations requires modernization of management methods and work organization as well as new competences and skills of workers. The Soviet ideology, which was deeply enrooted in political, social, professional activities, education and even personal life of Soviet citizens, suddenly appeared to be ineffective. This created a large uncertainty among those who were not flexible enough to reorient and train for a new profession or to adapt to the demands of modernity in other ways. This problem was the most acute for the older generation who were near the end of their professional career. It is not surprising that enterprises were more likely to invest in the education of young employees who are expected to work for a longer period and therefore to return larger outcomes. Following the logic of this statement, older people who had a great deal of work experience during the Soviet times but are less flexible under new conditions might appear to be less valuable workers and therefore less deserving. *I hypothesize that these two sorts of considerations related to the age of a person (need and desert) could balance each other in the minds of respondents when judging justice of earnings in Ukraine and leads to the not significant effect of age.*

According to the rule of "normative power of the factual" and the widespread traditional pattern of the gender socialization in Ukraine, I hypothesize that *the actual gender wage gap should be reflected in the distributive judgments of people, who are expected to ascribe higher earnings to men ceteris paribus.*

The need criterion is specified by family attributes such as one's marital status, employment status of spouse and number of children. The more individuals for whom one is responsible, the higher the financial need of the family, and, therefore, according to the need principle, the higher the income considered just for this person should be. Taking into account the incidence of poverty and informal economy in Ukraine, it is likely that *the need justice principle will dominate in the popular judgments*.

Some real life situations may present such combinations of personal characteristics that consideration of both need and merit justice principles would seem contradictory. The reconciliation of need and desert principles and overcoming the idea of their "trade-off relationship" was presented by K. E. Boulding (1962), who suggested that these two general principles underlie distributive justice judgments[10]. He argued that the potential conflict between two principles could be settled in the conception of a "social minimum," a level of resources below which nobody is allowed to fall, while considerations of desert are applied only when one treats the shares that are larger than a defined minimum. According to this statement, it is assumed that *there is some amount of income below which no income may be assessed as just, irrespective of the recipient's desert, and the merit principle first affects people's judgments when considering incomes that are larger than this minimum*. M. Alves and P. H. Rossi (1978) provide empirical evidence that there might also be a "social maximum," some amount of earnings over which no person should earn no matter how deserving (or needful) this person may be. So, the "social minimum" represents the fair amount of earnings the least deserving and least needful person should receive, while the "social maximum" relates to the just earnings of the most deserving and most needful individual.

Apart from personal characteristics, it is important to consider the features of the job-related environment, such as enterprise characteristics, which include financial condition of the place of employment, size of the company/enterprise, etc. Taking the specific context of a post-Soviet transforming economy into account, one of the most interesting and analytically important characteristics, the type of enterprise (state or private ownership), should be included in the analysis. Information on state or private sector belonging describes the objective differences in conditions of the economic environment in which employees are involved. Because higher salaries are generally paid in private organizations, *I hypothesize a conforming justice judging mechanism reflected in ascription of higher incomes for the fictitious employees working in private organizations*. Further, I hypothesize that *justice judgments depend, among others, on some kind of restrictions: if there exists an opportunity to acquire more resources, higher incomes are considered to be just*. If an

---

[10] He called them "principle of disalienation" (criterion of unit's need) and "principle of desert" (criterion of merit).

enterprise has a stable market position and obtains high revenues, those working at this enterprise deserve higher incomes as compared to employees working in less profitable companies. This statement could be considered an indirect application of the equality principle. That is, if the enterprise gains higher incomes, this profit should be distributed among the workers of this enterprise and not simply be appropriated by the owner. The opposite is also true: if the opportunity to get higher incomes is very improbable, for example, when an enterprise encounters the risk of insolvency, the workers of this enterprise should bear these common costs and consent to the lower wages.

Justice judgments depend not only upon the information on the situation provided to a respondent, but also upon his or her individual traits and personal life experience. Social scientists have found that people tend to build subjective images of larger society by generalizing from their own experience (Evans 2004: 4). From this point, a subjective assessment of just earnings is largely shaped by the individual's understanding of his or her direct social environment. If relying on the statement that the "is" situation defines, to some degree, the "should be" considerations of the people, then *the assessments of the just incomes provided by the respondents from low-income groups should, on average, be lower than those of more affluent individuals*. For example, just amount of earnings defined by the pensioners is expected to be lower than the earnings perceived as just by the working-age population. Similarly, people from rural areas, as compared to the city dwellers, would judge lower wages to be just, etc. Taking the immediate social environment as a reference point for one's own attitude is closely related to adaptation and cognitive dissonance reduction mechanisms. People would perhaps expect higher just wages for their work. However, if the disparities between reality and attitudes were to grow too large, people might become very distressed.

From the gender perspective, this effect combined with the effect of gender socialization may result in a "double discrimination" of female employees in the judgments of women. Since there is a gender wage gap in Ukraine and women are likely to compare their earnings to the earnings of other female colleagues (which is a natural process under conditions of labor market segregation), the reference earnings among female employees is likely to be lower than among men. Compounded by the effect of traditionalistic perception of male-breadwinner and female-housekeeper gender roles, *the just amount of earnings ascribed by a female respondent to a female employee can be even lower than the just amount of earnings ascribed to this employee by a male respondent.*

Respondent's age and educational attainment may also have an impact on popular justice attitudes. Because of work socialization during Soviet times, when returns to schooling were low and wages were not always correlated with investments in human capital, and owing to pensioners' poorer financial conditions under which individuals rationally seek redistribution (e.g., the need justice principle), *I expect older generation of citizens to pay more attention to the need and less to the desert-related information as compared to younger generation.*

On the other hand, the rational choice of those who have invested more in human capital than others is to advocate for the distribution according to the principle of desert. Therefore, I assume that *those with better education place more weight on desert-related characteristics as compared to respondents with lower educational attainment.*

Finally, some mechanisms of attitude formation may be better explored only by taking a comparative perspective. In looking at the order of factors that affect the formation of justice judgments in Ukraine and Germany and comparing them to the factors that actually define the level of earnings in each country, it is possible to assess the degree of correspondence between the "is" and "ought to be" situations. *Assuming the shaping effect of social context on the justice attitudes of people, it is likely that their justice judgments would reflect, to some degree, the existing rules of distribution.* However, considering the complex changes in the distribution system under transformation, I expect *the order of factors related to justice principles in Ukraine will not be in perfect correspondence with the country's present reality.*

CHAPTER SIX

RESEARCH DESIGN OF UKRAINIAN STUDY

In this chapter, I introduce the methodology used in the study on distributive justice attitudes in Ukraine including description of the factorial survey method, design of the questionnaire and collected data.

6.1 Factorial survey design

This study employs the factorial survey design to assess the value ascribed to desert, need and equality justice principles in the income evaluations of Ukrainians. The factorial survey is an innovative method that allows for the assessment of the weight of every justice principle in the process of the respondents' judgment of the justice of incomes. The specific design of the study makes it possible to estimate the strength of effects related to each of the dimensions relative to other effects and to compare them across different population groups.

My study of income distribution justice in Ukraine rests firmly on the methodological ground established in a German SOEP-Pretest study conducted in 2008 (Sauer et al. 2009b). The research design of the vignette module of both studies was developed by a team of German sociologists[1]. The vignette module of SOEP-Pretest 2008 was a template design for the vignette module of Omnibus 2009, which was conducted in Ukraine one year later. By the time of the fieldworks of Omnibus 2009, no analogous social science research involving the factorial survey technique had been conducted in Ukraine.

There are several reasons for relying on the survey design of this study. The most crucial is that using the same questionnaire design in Ukraine offers excellent prospects for a comparative study. Not less important is the content of vignette modules. Theoretically, a well-grounded and

---

[1] The team included T. Hinz, S. Liebig, K. Auspurg, and C. Sauer. The data collection was a part of the research project "The factorial survey as a method for measuring attitudes in population surveys" funded by the German Research Foundation in 2007-2010.

exhaustive list of vignette's dimensions takes a large number of factors into account. These factors are related to both: one's job as well as the most important demographic characteristics. Using the complete list of dimensions from the SOEP-Pretest study with some values adjusted for Ukraine makes it possible to test the full range of hypotheses formulated in this study.

In addition, the factorial survey design was thus far applied mostly for the measurement of distributive justice in small projects based on students' or other special groups' samples. In the SOEP-Pretest 2008, this method was tested on a representative sample in a large-scale survey. This positive experience suggests that the SOEP vignette module can be applied in other population surveys effectively.

6.1.1 Vignette dimensions

Selection of the dimensions and their values is the first step in vignette design strategy. The set of characteristics used in my study is presented in table 6.1. Every hypothetical person, whose income is evaluated by the respondents in terms of justice, is described by a certain combination of these characteristics.

The values of the age dimension in the SOEP-Pretest study included 25, 35, 45, and 55 years of age. However, some difficulties might have occurred regarding the age of 55 years in Ukraine because according to the Pension Provision Law of Ukraine[2], in 2009, 55 years was the retirement age for women (for men, it was 60 years). It means that after women attained this age they usually ended their professional career. That is why the value of "55 years old" was not relevant for the study in Ukraine at least for female fictitious persons; therefore, the range of age values was replaced by following: 25, 35, 40, and 50.

As mentioned below, because the list of values does not include the dimension of work experience[3], it is not possible to distinguish the pure meaning of the age dimension in this study. The age and sex of a fictitious person are considered, in this study, as important variables in the sense of

---

[2] Zakon Ukrajiny „Pro pensijne zabezpečennja" vid 05.11.1991
[3] The list of characteristics may be infinite. However, methodological findings of recent factorial survey studies show that the restriction is dictated by the capabilities of respondents, who begin to ignore some information in the vignettes if they become too complex (Auspurg, Hinz, Liebig 2009, Sauer et al. 2009a). The final list of characteristics chosen for a current study corresponds to the one used in the SOEP-Pretest 2008; this provides an opportunity for a comparative study.

the discrimination concept. These variables allow for testing for existence of justice inequalities in Ukraine.

Table 6.1. Dimensions and values

Dimensions	Values
Age	25, 35, 40, 50
Sex	Male, female
Marital status	Married with a non-working spouse, married with a working spouse, single
Education	Secondary education, vocational education, higher education
Occupation	Waiter, salesman, hairdresser, builder, bookkeeper, doctor, journalist, university professor, entrepreneur, lawyer
Income before taxes (UAH)	400, 600, 800, 1200, 1750, 3000, 4000, 5000, 8000, 15000
Children	No children, 1 child, 2 children, 3 children, 4 children
Work performance	Low, average, high achievements
Financial conditions of enterprise	High income, economically stable, on the verge of bankruptcy
State or private sector belonging of enterprise	Private enterprise, state enterprise

Independent variables characterizing number of children and marital status of a fictitious person reflect the need criteria in the study. Taking into account the real demographical situation in Ukraine with respect to number of children in a family, the value "no children" was weighted so that it appears twice as often as other categories[4].

Merit or desert considerations are presented in the list of dimensions by attributes of education, occupation, and work performance of a described person. In this study, I use three levels of education: secondary, vocational (technical or other education additional to the secondary education but not the university degree) and higher education.

The work performance of a vignette person was operationalized in three categories: low, average and high. In order to clarify what low or

[4] This procedure was realized by K. Auspurg (Universität Konstanz) analogously to the weighting of values in vignette module of the SOEP-Pretest 2008.

high work performance means to the respondents, a vignette person was compared with his/her colleagues. For example, a vignette pointing to a low performance indicated that a person does not work as well as her colleagues. A high performance was then expressed as "works better than her colleagues" and an average performance through "works as well as her colleagues."

With respect to occupational hierarchy, I proceed from the assumption that the prestige of the jobs is a kind of ordering of professions that is defined by the labor market rules, where the professions that require specific and rare skills and larger investment in education are placed at the top. Hence, ten different occupations were selected as deciles (plus one top occupation) on the prestige scale in the occupational prestige study conducted by Ukrainian sociologists S. Oksamytna and A. Patrakova (2007). In this study, respondents evaluated 31 different occupations in terms of being more or less prestigious using a five-term scale (1 – very high prestige, 0.5 – high prestige, 0 – middle prestige, -0.5 – low prestige, -1 – very low prestige).

At the next stage, a similar procedure was used to identify ten rungs of earnings (defined as deciles of actual earnings distribution and an extreme value) to use in vignettes. I employed four different sources of information to determine an existent income continuum in Ukraine: the three biggest national surveys – Omnibus-2007, "Ukrainian society" Monitoring 2008, European Social Survey 2006 – and the data provided by the State Statistics Service of Ukraine. Although the data they provide on incomes has a decisive nature for this study, these statistics are limited in what they reveal about real salaries in Ukraine. The problem in defining incomes is connected with the existing discrepancies between real and official income of people. The latter, which is usually reported in social surveys or official statistics, is almost always significantly lower than real income. This fact is a result of processes taking place in the transforming economy described in the previous section, namely shadow market functioning, tax evasion and corruption. Official statistics do not give exhaustive and accurate information about real incomes of the population because it does not take into account the aforementioned phenomena. I corrected the income ratings on the basis of analysis of job postings on the Internet with the intent of estimating the actual level of wages in Ukraine. Overall, 220 job postings were used for the correction of the salary continuum[5]. As a result,

---

[5] The information on salary amount was provided by the following web sites: http://alljob.com.ua/ (average salaries in 16 branches), http://job.ukr.net/, http://www.jobs.ua/ (for each Website 50 salaries in different branches and regions), http://job.bigmir.net/, http://www.job4you.com.ua/, http://work.com.ua/ and http://rabota-ukraine.com.ua/ (for each Website 30 salaries in different branches and regions).

three values (5000, 8000, 15000) were added to the list of income amounts instead of those that could be drawn from the empirical distributions of real incomes in the aforementioned data sets. The income dimension contains, therefore, the values that reflect real monthly earnings of Ukrainians albeit including extreme values much lower or higher than the average income.

As shown in previous studies, enterprise characteristics play a significant role in evaluation of just incomes, (e.g., Sauer et al. 2009a, Auspurg, Hinz, Liebig 2009). There are two attributes that describe an economic situation and a type of organization in vignettes: first, the sector (state or private organizations), and secondly, the financial state of an enterprise. Within the latter dimension, enterprises were described by using three values: enterprises making high revenues, economically stable organizations, and those on the verge of bankruptcy.

6.1.2 Vignette sample and questionnaire design

The systematically varying values constitute the object's descriptions, which are called vignettes. These vignettes are presented to the respondents in order to achieve an array of justice evaluations. Each of the respondents, instead of answering abstract questions regarding justice of certain inequalities, is asked to evaluate a certain number of vignettes. An example of a vignette composed from the values defined in the previous section follows:

A 35-year-old man with higher education works as a journalist in a state organization that receives high revenues. He does the work better than his colleagues. He is married with a working spouse and has no children. His monthly salary is **15000** UAH (before taxes).

How just or unjust do you think this salary is?

The salary is...

Too low					Just					Too high
-5	-4	-3	-2	-1	0	1	2	3	4	5
□	□	□	□	□	□	□	□	□	□	□

The respondents were asked to make their justice evaluations on a classical ordinal scale using 11 items. This scale ranges from -5, which corresponds to the lowest evaluation of income and describes the largest underreward, over 0 – the just reward, to 5, which indicates the largest overreward. This type of a scale was recently used in justice studies of Jasso, Opp (1997), Jann (2003), Auspurg et al. (2008), Auspurg, Hinz and Liebig (2009). The results of these studies suggest that this scale causes no difficulties in its application by respondents.

The introductory text before the vignette module highlights the fact that respondents should evaluate personal earnings of vignette persons (not total household incomes).

All possible vignettes composed of different values' combinations form a vignette universe. The vignette universe in this study comprised 1,166,400 fictitious descriptions of employees. In order to achieve reliable results, each of the respondents need not, of course, evaluate all of the vignettes. A proper sample that assures high quality of measurement should be drawn (see section 3.5.2). Based on the universe of realistic persons' descriptions, the sample of 240 vignettes was drawn using the fractional replication design[6] (see Alexander, Becker 1978). The sample of vignettes was based on the available list of vignettes after exclusion of implausible situations. The implausible situations are impossible combinations of fictitious person's characteristics, which according to previous methodological studies, provoke irritation among respondents and make them take further questions in the questionnaire not seriously (see Auspurg, Hinz, Liebig 2009). This can be reflected in unreliable and invalid results of the study. Since this is undesirable, I excluded the following combinations: lawyer, doctor and university professor with secondary or vocational education; bookkeeper with secondary education; income of a lawyer or a doctor – 400 UAH; income of a waiter, a salesman or a hairdresser – 15000 UAH.

By applying the two criteria of the D-efficient designs (orthogonality and level-balance), the vignettes were then combined into 20 decks, each consisting of 12 vignettes. The D-efficiency value of the vignette sample amounted to 96.5.

---

[6] The sampling procedure was realized by K. Auspurg (Universität Konstanz) analogously to the sampling design of the vignette module of the SOEP-Pretest 2008.

6.1.3 Pretest

The factorial survey method implies a rather demanding measurement procedure, which is reflected, among others, in the design of a questionnaire. Therefore, the pretest was supposed to give an impression on the perception of the vignettes by Ukrainians, who had no previous experience in answering similar questions. A selection of 12 vignettes was pretested on a sample of 30 students of the sociology department of the National Taras Ševčenko University of Kyiv in December 2008. The vignettes caused no problems of understanding. There were no critical remarks concerning formulation and presentation of vignettes among respondents. Based on the results of the pretest, the vignette module was approved and included into the main questionnaire of the Omnibus study 2009 without substantial changes[7].

6.2 The dataset: Omnibus 2009

The vignette module used in my study was part of a larger project – the Ukrainian Social Survey Omnibus 2009 conducted by Institute of Sociology of the National Academy of Sciences in Ukraine in collaboration with SOCIS social and marketing research organization (Institute of Sociology of the National Academy of Sciences of Ukraine 2009).

The Omnibus 2009 is a cross-section data on attitudes, perceptions, and behavior of Ukrainian citizens. Previous waves of the Omnibus survey took place in 2006 and 2007. Each time, representative samples of the adult population were surveyed using both previously posed and novel questions.

The respondent sample consists of the 1799 citizens of Ukraine (18 years and older) that were selected using geographically stratified quota-sampling as proportional to size of regions in Ukraine. The respondents were selected using the quotas to represent the age, gender and education structure of the population in the region. These were computed based on the Ukrainian general census of the population in 2001 (Vseukrajins'kyj perepys naselennja 2001). The description of the sample is presented in table 6.2.

In total, the questionnaire consisted of 252 questions (40 questionnaire pages). It comprised one of the twenty decks (a selection of 12 vignettes)

---

[7] One sentence was added in the introduction paragraph explaining the task of respondents.

and a large number of questions on political, economic, cultural, health and other issues, including socio-demographic information. An advantage of the large survey is availability of the data on a number of issues, which allows for a comprehensive analysis of justice attitudes of different population groups of diverse socio-demographic characteristics.

Table 6.2 Description of the sample (N = 1799)

	Omnibus 2009, Respondents 18 years old and older	Census 2001, Citizens 17 years old and older
Age		
Mean	46	
Std. Deviation	16.98	
Min	18	
Max	88	
Gender (%)		
Male	45.1	46.3
Female	54.9	53.7
Education (%)		
Primary education or less	24.4	25
Secondary general and vocational education	61.9	59.9
Higher (including bachelor) education or scientific degree	13.7	14.6

Questionnaire versions were randomly assigned to the respondents and every respondent evaluated one deck so that multiple ratings (from 83 to 96) were received on each vignette. The randomization check summary is presented in table 6.3, which shows a number of respondents evaluating each deck by respondents' socio-demographic characteristics (column percentages are in parentheses). The last row of the table shows the p-values indicating no relationship between decks and respondent characteristics such as gender, education or age. Each deck was evaluated at least once per administrative unit[8]. There was no variation of vignettes' order in the decks.

---

[8] In total, 26 units were defined: 24 oblasts, AR Crimea and Kyiv city.

Table 6.3 Randomization check

Deck	Male	Female	Secondary and less	Vocational	Higher	Mean age	N
1	42 (5.19)	54 (5.47)	56 (5.15)	22 (4.77)	18 (7.32)	46.5	96
2	42 (5.19)	46 (4.66)	50 (4.6)	25 (5.42)	13 (5.28)	46.2	88
3	45 (5.56)	43 (4.36)	58 (5.34)	21 (4.56)	9 (3.66)	45.5	88
4	33 (4.07)	52 (5.27)	53 (4.88)	21 (4.56)	11 (4.47)	46	85
5	33 (4.07)	55 (5.57)	57 (5.24)	24 (5.21)	7 (2.85)	49.1	88
6	40 (4.94)	51 (5.17)	52 (4.78)	24 (5.21)	15 (6.1)	43	91
7	33 (4.07)	59 (5.98)	59 (5.43)	22 (4.77)	10 (4.07)	46.3	92
8	37 (4.57)	54 (5.47)	53 (4.88)	25 (5.42)	13 (5.28)	49.7	91
9	48 (5.93)	45 (4.56)	60 (5.52)	22 (4.77)	11 (4.47)	45.9	93
10	42 (5.19)	49 (4.96)	55 (5.06)	20 (4.34)	16 (6.5)	46.6	91
11	45 (5.56)	44 (4.46)	46 (4.23)	29 (6.29)	14 (5.69)	45.8	89
12	45 (5.56)	44 (4.46)	53 (4.88)	23 (4.99)	13 (5.28)	46.6	89
13	40 (4.94)	54 (5.47)	62 (5.7)	19 (4.12)	13 (5.28)	45	94
14	46 (5.68)	45 (4.56)	51 (4.69)	21 (4.56)	19 (7.72)	45.5	91
15	42 (5.19)	51 (5.17)	54 (4.97)	28 (6.07)	11 (4.47)	44.2	93
16	43 (5.31)	46 (4.66)	58 (5.34)	21 (4.56)	9 (3.66)	45.4	89
17	42 (5.19)	44 (4.46)	52 (4.78)	27 (5.86)	7 (2.85)	44.8	86
18	27 (3.33)	56 (5.67)	49 (4.51)	21 (4.56)	12 (4.88)	47.4	83
19	46 (5.68)	43 (4.36)	52 (4.78)	26 (5.64)	11 (4.47)	47.6	89
20	39 (4.81)	52 (5.27)	57 (5.24)	20 (4.34)	14 (5.69)	42.2	91
p	0.286		0.932			0.499	

For categorical variables (gender, education) the p-values are taken from Chi^2-tests; for continuous variable (age) p-values from joint test of the equality of means across decks is presented.

CHAPTER SEVEN

CONTEXTUAL PERSPECTIVE: DISTRIBUTIVE JUSTICE EVALUATIONS IN UKRAINE

7.1 Descriptive evidence

As an initial step, I present a general descriptive analysis of the income justice evaluations. Figure 1 presents the distribution of all 21549 statements that were collected for the vignettes from 1797 respondents. Almost half (50.8%) of evaluations about income justice was expressed using the scale from -5 to -1, which corresponds to the statement "the salary is too low". Moreover, 25.3% of all judgments have been based on the extreme value of -5. Obviously, about half of the estimated real continuum of wages in Ukraine is evaluated by the respondents as too low, and a quarter of all earning amounts have received the lowest assessment.

The distribution of answers presented in figure 1 resembles censored distribution. In our case, respondents would perhaps sometimes choose even lower values to assess earnings they perceived to be unjustly too low if the scale would have permitted it. The problems caused by censored data should be taken into account in the further analysis.

A next peculiar point is that in my study, 21.8% of responses refer to zero value, which corresponds to the judgment "the income is just," making it the second most frequent answer category. Apart from these two dominant values (-5 and 0), the respondents' ratings are more or less equally distributed across the rest of the answer categories.

The high frequency of the zero-assessments ("the income is just") may have at least two sources of origin. First, it is likely to be a common tendency of respondents to select middle categories of the ordinal scale. Second, it may be a result of the operation of the psychological mechanism known as "belief in a just world," which is a "belief that people get what they deserve and deserve what they get." This mechanism serves a protective function defending the individual psychologically against the possibility of an undeserved negative outcome (Appelbaum,

Lenon, Aber 2006). If I exclude the three lowest values (400, 600, and 800 UAH) of the income dimension from analysis, the distribution of answer categories would be similar to those of other methodologically similar Western studies (e.g., Sauer et al. 2009a, 2009b, Auspurg et al. 2008, Alves, Rossi 1978) with a zero value ("just income" ratings) appearing in 29.5% of vignette evaluations and other answer categories present in the assessments of respondents more or less equally (figure 7.2).

Figure 7.1 Income justice evaluations, in percent

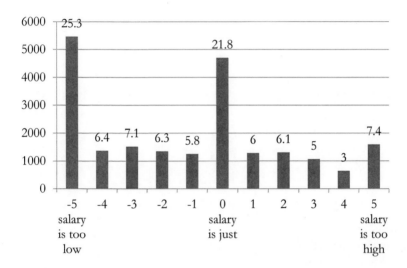

Six out of ten earnings used in the vignettes on average were rated as unfairly low (table 3). The fact that standard deviations grow together with amount of earnings presented in the vignettes demonstrates that there is less consensus among respondents about justice of higher incomes than there is about the lower ones.

Figure 7.2 Income justice evaluations (incomes ranged from 1200 to 15000 UAH), in percent

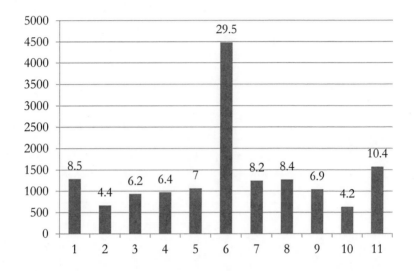

Table 7.1 Mean justice evaluations depending on incomes indicated in vignettes

Income	Mean justice evaluation	Std. Deviation
400	-4.41	1.438
600	-4.1	1.630
800	-3.74	1.813
1200	-2.5	2.151
1750	-1.89	2.251
3000	-0.25	2.115
4000	0.16	2.196
5000	0.72	2.165
8000	1.71	2.282
15000	2.96	2.274

7.2 General model

The general model to be assessed aims at studying the effect of the factors in the vignettes on the justice evaluations of Ukrainians. To assess the weight of every such factor, I calculated a multiple regression linear model with the justice judgments as dependent variables and the characteristics of the vignette (age, sex, occupation, etc.) as independent variables. Each respondent had to make 12 judgments (these judgments lead to the samples size of N=21549 in the regression analysis). These evaluations are not completely independent, and there is some degree of intrapersonal correlations between justice ratings. Under these conditions, the estimated standard error of the coefficients can be distorted. Thus, it is strongly recommended to account for possible clusters of the evaluations (Hox, Kreft, Hermkens 1991).

There is intense debate among social scientists concerning the most appropriate and accurate procedures for analysis of data resulting from factorial surveys. One of the issues is whether one may apply procedures for continuous variables to ordinal variables as far as the most widespread scale used for collecting respondents' judgments in factorial surveys is ordinal (ranging as a rule from 6 to 11 points). Scholars have provided several arguments in favor of application of the least squares method to ordinal variables if the number of categories is quite large (Bentler, Chou 1987). Thus, a number of papers using the factorial survey data provide analyses of linear regressions based on Huber standard errors and consequently take the hierarchical structure of the data into account (e.g., Auspurg, Hinz, Liebig 2009; Liebig, Mau 2005a; Jasso, Opp 1997). However, as already mentioned, potential difficulties may arise if the data I address in this study are censored.

For the purpose of appropriate model selection and a robustness check of the substantive results, different models were tested. The two principal criteria of the model selection were taking a structure of the data into account and simplifying the interpretation of results. Several models were estimated. Among them were the Huber-Regression, ordinal logistic regression, multinomial logistic regression and Tobit model. The regression coefficients of all models estimated showed the same direction and mostly the same significance of effects, which led to similar conclusions on relationships among variables. For purposes of comparison, I present two models here: an OLS-Regression with robust standard errors, which permits the clearest interpretation of results, and a random-intercept Tobit model, which is considered the most accurate model for being specially designed for the multi-level censored data.

Table 4 presents the estimation results of the OLS-Regression with robust standard errors where the respondents are treated as clustering units (model 1) and a random-intercept Tobit model with respondents seen as a second level units (model 2). The latter model is preferred in the following deeper analysis for the reason that it is considered more accurate even though it is more complex and perhaps somewhat more complicated for the interpretation.

The general equation for the random-intercept Tobit model (table 7.2, model 2) may be written as follows:

$$y_{ij}^* = \beta_{0j} + \sum_{k=1}^{K} \beta_k x_{kij} + e_{ij} + u_{0j}$$

$$
\begin{aligned}
y_{ij} &= -5 && \text{for } y_{ij}^* \leq -5 \\
y_{ij} &= y_{ij}^* && \text{for } -5 < y_{ij}^* < 5 \\
y_{ij} &= 5 && \text{for } y_{ij}^* \geq 5
\end{aligned}
$$

Where $i = 1, 2, ..., I$ – refers to the units of the level 1 (vignettes), $j = 1, 2, ..., J$ – to the units of the level 2 (respondents), and $k = 1, 2, ..., K$ – to the number of a variable, which corresponds to a vignette dimension x; e_{ij} is a level 1 error term, and u_{0j} is a level 2 error term; β_{0j} is a random intercept. The dependent variable is a justice evaluation of a vignette.

Positive or negative signs of the regression coefficients show the direction of influence. A positive sign means that the earnings tend to be evaluated as rather too high if a respective value is presented in a vignette instead of a reference category or in the case of a metric variable (for example, logarithm of income), the justice evaluation is likely to be done rather on the overpaid side of the scale as a characteristic's value rises. The logarithm of earnings was entered into the regression because there are theoretical reasons to expect diminishing utility of earnings at the higher margin of the income continuum. It is widely acknowledged that people are less sensitive to small income changes when income amounts become considerably large. This mathematical transformation improved the explanation power of the OLS model and substantially increased the value of R^2 from 0.49 to 0.60. According to the coefficients presented in table 7.2, it becomes clear that the major part of variation in ratings is accounted for by the income dimension. This is not surprising since it is this dimension that represents amount of earnings evaluated by Ukrainians in terms of justice.

Table 7.2 OLS-Regression with robust standard errors (Huber-Regression) and random-intercept Tobit regression

	Model 1 (OLS)		Model 2 (Tobit)			
	Coefficient	Std. Err.	Coefficient	Std. Err.	Marg. effects	Std. Err.
Age	0.001	0.001	0.001	0.002	0.001	0.001
Female sex[1]	0.183***	0.024	0.249***	0.035	0.131***	0.019
Marital status[2]						
- working spouse	0.234***	0.032	0.349***	0.043	0.184***	0.023
- single	-0.009	0.032	-0.019	0.052	-0.010	0.023
Education[3]						
- vocational	0.100**	0.036	0.098	0.052	0.052	0.027
- higher	-0.044	0.038	-0.103	0.053	-0.054	0.028
Occupation[4]						
- salesman	-0.114*	0.052	-0.175*	0.053	-0.092*	0.040
- hairdresser	-0.022	0.056	0.028	0.076	0.015	0.040
- builder	-0.478***	0.056	-0.711***	0.076	-0.374***	0.040
- bookkeeper	-0.249***	0.058	-0.260**	0.077	-0.137**	0.041
- doctor	-0.423***	0.068	-0.531***	0.088	-0.279***	0.046
- journalist	-0.271***	0.055	-0.363***	0.074	-0.191***	0.039
- professor	-0.233***	0.066	-0.286**	0.087	-0.151**	0.046
- entrepreneur	-0.389***	0.054	-0.516***	0.076	-0.271***	0.040
- lawyer	-0.485***	0.064	-0.571***	0.086	-0.300***	0.045
Log of income	2.184***	0.019	2.897***	0.018	1.525***	0.009
Children[5]						
- one child	-0.314***	0.039	-0.385***	0.053	-0.203***	0.028
- two children	-0.488***	0.039	-0.584***	0.052	-0.307***	0.027
- three children	-0.695***	0.040	-0.935***	0.053	-0.492***	0.028
- four children	-0.794***	0.041	-1.163***	0.054	-0.612***	0.028
Performance[6]						
- average	-0.349***	0.032	-0.468***	0.043	-0.246***	0.023
- high	-0.433***	0.032	-0.605***	0.043	-0.319***	0.023
Enterprise[7]						
- economically stable	0.022	0.030	0.091*	0.043	0.048*	0.023
- on the verge of bankruptcy	0.222***	0.033	0.285***	0.044	0.150***	0.023
Private sector[8]	-0.072**	0.029	-0.076*	0.038	-0.040*	0.020
Constant	-17.312***	0.165	-23.035***	0.179		
R[2]	0.60		.			
Respondents	1797		1797			
Vignettes	21 549		21 549			
Estimated random intercept std. dev.	.	.	1.270	0.029		
Estimated level 1 (vignettes) std. dev.	.	.	2.396	0.016		
Intraclass correlation coefficient	.	.	0.219	0.008		

* p < 0.05, ** p < 0.01, *** p < 0.001

Note to table 7.2: Dependent variable is an estimation of the just income made by respondents on the 11-term scale with values from -5 (the income is too low) to 5 (the income is too high). The unit of analysis is a vignette, not a respondent. For the random-intercept Tobit model the Wald Chi^2(25) = 27898.86, p<0.001. Effects on the latent variable and the average marginal effects on the truncated variable are presented. Reference categories: [1] male, [2] married with a non-working spouse, [3] secondary education, [4] waiter, [5] no children, [6] low, [7] high revenues, [8] state sector.

More importantly, the respondents paid attention to almost all of the characteristics that were used in the vignettes. This indicates that personal, family and enterprise characteristics of the described fictitious persons indeed affected justice evaluations of Ukrainians. Since the characteristics attributed to vignette persons were not equally important for these evaluations, I may conclude that the justice principles that underlie every vignette dimension played unequal role for the distributive justice judgments of respondents.

The regression coefficients presented in table 7.2 reveal the direction and significance of the relationship between just earnings and respective characteristics of the vignette persons. Practically all the effects are in the expected direction.

In general, Ukrainian citizens consider higher earnings to be just for male workers, those occupying more prestigious jobs, those with more children, those who perform better and those working in private organizations or organizations with better financial situations. According to the respondents' answers, those employees who have another breadwinner in a household should earn less compared to singles or those who are married with a non-working spouse. The effects of age and educational attainment of a vignette person are not significant. Further analysis treats these and other empirical findings in more detail.

7.3 How unjust is the gender wage gap really?

A positive sign of the female sex dummy represents a shift in judgment in the direction of overpayment. This means that under all equal conditions, men tend to be rated rather underpaid in comparison to women. The positive highly significant coefficient related to the sex of a fictitious person shows that, in general, respondents were evaluating the unjustly low wages more radically when confronted with descriptions of male employees who received low wages. Similarly, people were more reluctant to acknowledge that explicitly high incomes were unjustly too high if the situation concerned a male fictitious person as compared to a female. The empirical findings demonstrate that the gender wage gap is indeed considered just in Ukraine.

I explore the situation from a more detailed gender perspective in order to understand whether women and men share the same views on the gender-specified income justice. In other words, I seek to determine whether male and female respondents equally discriminate women with respect to fair levels of income. I thus divided the sample into two subgroups on the basis of respondents' sex and computed the mean justice evaluations of earnings for two groups of respondents (male and female) depending on sex of the fictitious person (figure 7.3).

Figure 7.3. Mean justice evaluations of income for male and female fictitious persons

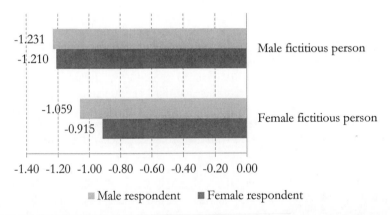

A test for comparison of means reveals an expected difference between the mean evaluations of just earnings of male and female respondents (t-test, $p<0.05$): both consider female fictitious persons to deserve less earnings for their work as compared to male vignette persons while controlling for all other characteristics. Moreover, it appears that Ukrainian women discriminate against themselves even more than men do (t-test, $p<0.05$). Interestingly, the empirical results of the study on justice attitudes conducted by B. Jann (2003) revealed the same effect in Switzerland. Male respondents believe that women have to earn less than men, but what they consider fair for female employees is significantly higher than the earnings considered to be just for them by female respondents. This finding may seem surprising, but it is nevertheless in line with the assumption that the socialization effect may supplement the effect of a referential structure comparison. In other words, the just gender wage gap in the answers of the female respondents is likely to be a result of the operation of two mechanisms: first, the socialization mechanism, which assures the acquisition of the understanding of traditional gender roles ("male-breadwinner" and "female-housekeeper"), and second, the inclination to judge a society based on subjective experience and perception of one's direct social environment. Under conditions of labor market segregation, women often have no other choice but to compare their income with the mean income of their reference group, which consists of other women. Under these circumstances the double effect of women's discrimination may be observed: first, women believe they should earn less than men, and, second, what they expect as a just wage is significantly lower than what men ascribe to them.

Furthermore, it is likely that apart from putting less effort on the career development of women because of popular traditional gender roles, people in Ukraine adapt to existing gender inequalities, accept them as an objectively given reality and accordingly adjust their justice attitudes. Both men and women justify gender inequality with respect to earnings because it is common practice that the husband should earn more than his wife. Even in social surveys where direct questions about gender inequality are asked, a substantial part of the population demonstrates discriminating attitudes. For instance, according to the WVS 2011 almost half of the population (48.1%) disagreed with the strong statement "If a woman earns more money than her husband, it is almost certain to cause problems", while the rest of respondents either agreed (21.5%), or were ambiguous and chose the alternative "neither agree, nor disagree" (30.4%). Similarly, the data of ESS in 2010 demonstrate the broad acceptance of traditional gender roles: 71.3% of respondents agreed or agreed strongly with the statement "Women should be prepared to cut down on paid work for sake of family", 9.5% disagreed (of which only 2.4% disagreed strongly), and 19.2% neither agreed nor disagreed.

Since people's values do not contradict real gender inequalities, respondents have almost no incentives to deeply reflect on this state of affairs and they simply do not perceive gender differences as an unjust discrimination.

Based on the theoretical elaborations of G. Jasso (2007) and using the modified formula of K. Auspurg and A. Jäckle (2012), I computed mean just incomes for male and female fictitious persons. An application of a respective formula[1] yields 4159 UAH as an average just wage for a male employee, and respectively 3746 UAH for a female employee. A

---

[1] The description of the formula is presented in section 7.8.

difference of 413 UAH means just female wages are about 10% lower than the just wages of men ceteris paribus.

7.4 The need and desert principles

I turn now to consider the effects of justice principles of need and desert. As mentioned above, the need principle of justice is represented in this study by the characteristics of marital status and number of children of a vignette person. The observed response pattern suggests that being married with a working spouse makes people believe that the financial needs of fictitious people decrease and, as a result, the assessments of just income tend to be more positive. That is, respondents consider married working couples to be rather overpaid in comparison to single persons or persons married to unemployed spouses. In addition, respondents certainly take into account the number of children indicated in the vignettes while defining the just incomes. Larger family size leads people believe that a higher level of income is just for a fictitious person. Increment in number of children causes increment in just earnings, and it is also essential to note that the effect of this dimension is the strongest in the model (apart from the income dimension).

Apparently, people do not seem to distinguish between duties of the state and the employer when ascribing the responsibility of satisfying their basic financial needs to a generalized abstract body (state, employer, "people at the top," etc.). This answer pattern is likely to reflect a stable idea remained from the Soviet time regarding the state as the only employer and sole guarantor of social security. The fundamental view on organization of major social institutions and their functions seems to have remained in modern Ukraine from the Soviet times: people expect to receive all means for sustainability of their households from the state, which is pervasive across all formal social relations. The social security system, labor remuneration, and generally any contribution to individual welfare was formerly controlled by the state through various mechanisms. The breakup of the Soviet Union sharply changed the role of the state; however, the perception of its duties may still be seen in the population opinion polls. People feel strongly that the state should provide guaranteed jobs and a minimal standard of living[2]. The perception of centralized

---

[2] According to European Social Survey in 2008, on a scale of 1 to 10, 64% of Ukrainian respondents marked the last extreme value that corresponded to a statement "providing job for everyone is entirely government's responsibility." For comparison, this value was chosen by only 18% of respondents in Germany.

"vertical" power and subordination seems to be reflected in justice attitudes of Ukrainians who expect that employers alone must take care of the financial wellbeing of households. I suggest that the effect of presence of children in a family will have the largest power in the model until the boundaries between state and employer responsibilities with respect to securing the appropriate standard of living are not drawn distinctly.

The desert principle is presented in this study by the dimensions of educational attainment, occupation, and performance at workplace. Under application of this principle by respondents, one expects that the higher occupational prestige, education, and employee's performance is, the higher just income ascribed to a vignette person would be. Ukrainians judge the justice of incomes regardless of the educational attainment involved in the vignette. This finding leads to the recognition of a remarkable difference in the judgment of income justice in Ukraine and West European countries. In studies of the latter, educational attainment is considered by people in their justice judgments, and the basic human capital theory statement provides a valid explanation for this. I assumed that Ukrainian reality marked by the weak linkage between educational system and labor market may affect the justice judgments of people. Respondents' answer patterns imply that people perceive the important human capital to be acquired not as much through the formal education as through other mechanisms.

As far as the specific features of the post-Soviet transformation process are concerned, the relevant professional qualifications and skills are very often acquired outside formal educational institutions. This seems to be one of the most plausible reasons that people disregard information on the education of a vignette person in their justice judgments. Analyzing the ISJP 1991 and 1996 data, Russian sociologists state: "In the turbulent times of transition it is not so much better-educated people who have advantages in the market, but people with other resources – entrepreneurial talents, personal initiative, or vocational skills – who can find customers who would pay hard cash, be it perhaps through car servicing or work in construction" (Stephenson, Khakhulina 2000: 85). The vignette evaluations of Ukrainians suggest that people associate such important vocational skills not necessarily with attainment of official education. The channels to obtain such skills can be diverse: from the on-the-job training to taking specialized professional courses.

Regression coefficients presented in table 7.2 illustrate the absence of consecutive order in evaluation of just incomes according to prestige of occupations. The more prestigious occupation of university professor has a substantially smaller magnitude of negative effect than does the less prestigious occupation of builder. In the most recent study of professional prestige in 2007, Ukrainian sociologists S. Oksamytna and A. Patrakova (2007) have noticed an increase in the prestige level of the builder profession in the past decade and have considered the reason for this may lie in the lack of qualified workers observed during the building boom of the last years and in the growth of wages in the construction sector. The "normative power of factual" thesis makes it plausible to assume that the justice evaluations of Ukrainians reflect their expectations towards the actual earnings for the considered occupations. Referring to the prevalence of informal economic behavior in Ukraine, one may derive a further hypothesis that the effect of occupation is, in turn, determined by an unobserved variable, which relates to the scope of opportunity for a given occupation to put into practice some kind of informal economic behavior and, in this way, to secure an additional income or a complementary profit to a defined salary. The coefficients relating to the occupations of bookkeeper and university professor make the mentioned hypothesis worth testing in future research. There is, of course, a possibility of exceptions. For example, the occupation of journalist usually implies that the earnings of an employee are composed of basic rates and supplementary fees for a defined volume of work. Therefore, a relatively small salary could be considered just if the amount of additional earnings is supposed to increase the overall monthly income to a fair level.

The third characteristic relating to the desert principle of justice is work performance, which describes the productivity of an employee. The results of my study provide clear empirical evidence for a strong relationship between this characteristic and the assessed level of just earnings. In other words, there is a distinct direct correspondence between the level of occupational achievements of a fictitious person and the amount of his or her earnings considered to be just. This finding is consistent with the research results related to the application of the merit principle in many other countries, and it points to the universality of the desert justice principle. In Ukraine, the effect of work performance on the amount of just earnings is noticeably the strongest among the desert-related characteristics in the model. It corresponds to the assumption that in contemporary post-Soviet transforming states, these kinds of human capital measures are more relevant as compared to formal educational attainment and occupational prestige.

I may conclude that the major idea of the human capital theory is reflected in the judgments of respondents, although the measure of the human capital is not formal educational attainment but rather work performance in this case.

7.5 Characteristics of enterprises

Following the argument on limited opportunities to receive higher incomes described in the theoretical part of this paper, I turn now to the analysis of two enterprise characteristics that were presented in the vignettes. From Table 7.2, one may derive the conclusion that financial conditions of an enterprise are taken into consideration by the respondents: the coefficients illustrate the relationship in the expected direction. According to the justice judgments of Ukrainians, if an enterprise receives higher revenues, it should pay higher salaries to its employees. If an indicated enterprise, by contrast, is described as being on the verge of bankruptcy, the categories relating to justice judgments are more likely to be found on the right part of the scale – "the salary is too high." Consequently, respondents are likely to believe that high profits as well as burdens (acceptance of lower incomes for the sake of an enterprise people work at) should be distributed among the workers of this enterprise. In compliance with this statement, respondents expect higher incomes for employees of private organizations as compared to those of state enterprises. This could also serve as another argument in favor of the aforementioned thesis, which suggests that the actual state of affairs in the country shapes, to some degree, people's views on what should be considered just. These two findings suggest that people adjust their justice attitudes to the actual situation and define just incomes in accordance with the amount of resources available.

The economic crisis of 2009 might have bolstered the importance of enterprises' revenue as described in the vignettes. Since many employers in 2009 reduced wages and retired their workers as a reaction to the economic crisis, the consideration "it is better to get less than nothing" was likely preferable for many employees. Accordingly, respondents who perceived the experience of their family members and friends who lost their jobs were likely to be less demanding with respect to earnings perceived as fair. Therefore, considering vignette persons who work at economically unstable enterprises, Ukrainian respondents evaluated their just incomes less severely and expected smaller amounts of earnings for them.

7.6 Social minimum and social maximum

In the context of my study, one of the crucial questions posed is how principles of desert and need relate to each other. Empirical findings suggest that the need criterion plays the most significant role in the process of judging just earnings. The question is whether the need principle generally plays a decisive role in defining the just incomes in Ukraine or if this holds true only when certain conditions apply. Most of the findings described below were presented in my previous work (see Gatskova 2013). In the following, I refine the analysis and place the interpretation of results into the context of a broader discussion.

Proceeding from the thesis of Boulding (1962) that desert and need principles complement each other and that the desert principle first comes into play when earnings larger than the necessary minimum are considered, I assess an average amount of earnings below which no income is considered to be just by Ukrainian respondents (irrespective of vignette person's characteristics). This amount of income is called a "social minimum." To uncover the complementary relation of the two principles, I test an assumption that the desert principle affects people's justice judgments stronger after incomes that are larger than this minimum are considered. On the other hand, there are incomes that are considered to be too large irrespective of one's merits and needs. This ceiling is called the "social maximum."

The idea of social minimum and maximum is twofold: first, it can be considered in absolute terms (social minimum and maximum defined for all individuals in a society), and second, it may be applied separately for different population groups. In this sense, social minimum and maximum can specially be defined for women, people with higher education, families with four children, employees representing certain profession, etc. The application of need and desert justice principles leads to a shift of respective boundaries of social minimum and social maximum in every particular case.

Some support for the speculation on social minimum and social maximum can be derived from the descriptive analysis of the data, which show that practically all (96%) respondents evaluated vignette persons as underpaid when the minimum value of income dimension (400 UAH) appeared in a vignette and tended, in the overwhelming majority of cases (76% of respondents), to evaluate as overpaid those vignette persons who received the highest earnings (15000 UAH). To put it in other words, the justice ratings tend to be made on the negative part of the scale ("the salary is too small") irrespective of all other characteristics of a vignette person if the smallest earnings amounts are considered. Respectively, the highest income tends to be evaluated as "too high" no matter what combinations of other values appeared in a vignette person's description. These findings are in line with those found by Alves and Rossi (1978) in the USA. Scholars have shown that people tend to take considerations of social minimum and maximum into account when they judge the justice of earnings.

Social minimum was defined as a just income of the least deserving and least needful individual. I defined as such those fictitious individuals who were described as married to working spouses, having no children and showing low performance at their workplaces[3]. With this combination of values, the mean just earnings is supposed to reflect the basic fair amount of income under which no member of society should receive, irrespective of how negligible his or her needs and deserts may be. Out of 21549 vignettes used in the study, 641 cases contained defined combination of values. In turn, the combination of values describing the most deserving fictitious person – married to a non-working spouse, having 4 children and marked by high achievements in the workplace – appear 712 times. The computed just amounts of earnings for each of the groups are presented in table 7.3.

Table 7.3 Assessments of just wages

	N	Mean just wages (UAH)
Least deserving	641	2519
Most deserving	712	5370
Person having no children	7102	3266
Person having 1 child	3593	3778
Person having 2 children	3679	3907
Person having 3 children	3600	4552
Person having 4 children	3590	4910
Person with low performance	7192	3464
Person with average performance	7177	4041
Person with high performance	7195	4342
Married, non-working spouse	7453	4128
Married, working spouse	6826	3610

Source: Gatskova (2013: 238).

---

[3] I have taken into account the most salient need and desert criteria (number of family members and work performance), involving other characteristics would have considerably decreased the number of vignettes selected for the further analysis.

If the assessment of mean just earnings for the least deserving individual is taken as a reference point, one may observe the combined result of application of the need and desert principles reflected in the substantial increase of mean just earnings of the fictitious person specified as the most deserving. Additionally, it is possible to trace the increment of just income amounts as soon as needs or deserts of a vignette person grow. According to the data of this study, the minimum just value associated with the least deserving person is equal to 2519 UAH, which exceeds the official subsistence minimum in 2009 provided by the State Statistics Service of Ukraine by 3.5 times.

The next task was to test the assumption concerning conditions of application of the need and desert justice principles and their weight for justice judgments of Ukrainians. The relative strength of the two respective factors (number of children and level of achievements of an employee) was compared across two models. The first model related to values from 1200 to 5000 of income continuum[4]. The second model was based on the vignettes that treated values higher than the assessed maximum just income (6285). These are the last two highest income values of this study – 8000 and 15000 UAH. The relative weight of the factors within each of the models is presented in figure 7.4.

Figure 7.4 Relative weight of the factors in models computed for the 1200-5000 income continuum and for the two highest values (8000 and 15000), z-values

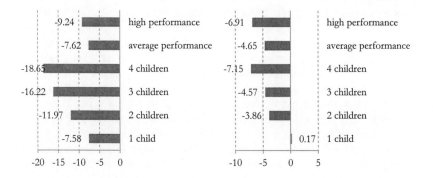

---

[4] I excluded three lower values (400, 600, 800 UAH) from this analysis due to very high proportion of extreme negative assessments.

It is remarkable that in the model where only high incomes are considered, the factor of high work performance plays a relatively greater role than the presence of three children in a family, in sharp contrast to the initial model, where presence of two or more children in a family was a decisive factor to increase the just amount of income. The effect of one child in a family with large incomes on just earnings loses its significance in the second model. On the other hand, the level of achievements at the workplace becomes somewhat higher weight if larger income amounts are considered. This finding is in line with the speculation of Boulding (1962) concerning the complementation of need and desert principles: the merit considerations first come into play after income amounts that are larger than social minimum are treated.

Summing up, the data suggest that the need justice principle dominates in the judgments of respondents in Ukraine, especially if incomes that do not suffice to ensure a decent standard of living for a described vignette family are considered. As far as incomes larger than social minimum are examined, the desert justice principle gains in importance.

The tendency discovered through this analysis allows one to assume that under consideration of much higher income values than I have selected for this study, the effect of the number of children will diminish and, at some point, is likely to become insignificant. The continuum of income values chosen for this study is apparently somewhat skewed to the left and this is the most probable reason for the skewed distribution of overall vignette assessments. This also means that the actual official incomes in Ukraine that served as a basis for the selection of income values for this study are generally considered extremely low and do not correspond to the expectations of Ukrainians about just amounts of earnings. Empirical data provide reasons to expect that much higher income values chosen for the vignettes would stimulate other answer patterns of Ukrainians. Namely, people would probably not only be led by the considerations of social security and "care" about large families by transmitting the function of a state to an employer, but would, to a higher degree, pay attention to the job-related characteristics. The present answer patterns of respondents point to a general social insecurity of the Ukrainian population.

Furthermore, the findings concerning social minimum and social maximum suggest that people regard the just incomes in relative terms. This means that irrespective of one's merits or needs, Ukrainians have a certain view on a just range of incomes. This range of incomes begins with a social minimum at the bottom of income distribution and ends with a social maximum at the top. Every individual in a society may have his or her own vision of social minimum and maximum, but there is also a considerable consensus about the amount of minimum just wage among citizens. The reference point for the definition of the minimum just earnings is the actual social context. The fact that people in Ukraine regard employers responsible for the adjustments of earnings to employees' needs points to the patriarchal view of the employer. This means, that the old Soviet perception of getting everything from "people at the top" is still present among people. This perception was formed during Soviet times, when social policy to a large extent was realized through a workplace[5].

7.7 Differences in justice judgments across population groups

I assumed the effect of the socio-demographic characteristics of respondents on their distributive justice attitudes. In this section, I test this assumption by considering the differences in justice judgments across various population groups. I focus on the differences in attitudes among age cohorts, educational groups, and among citizens residing in different regions of Ukraine and in urban or rural areas.

7.7.1 Justice evaluations across age cohorts

I start with a test of the assumption that because of differing socialization experiences, younger people in Ukraine pay more attention to the human capital-related characteristics such as education, occupational prestige and work performance and less to the need principle as compared to older generations. I tested this hypothesis in the article published before (see Gatskova 2013). In this section, I mostly rely on the findings reported in the article.

As a first step of the hypothesis test, I divided the sample into two groups. The first group, labeled "younger generation," consists of respondents who were under 30 years old as the USSR collapsed. The second group is called "older generation," and it includes those who were older than 30 at this time and hence had spent their most important years of work socialization in the old system. Because Ukraine was only 18 years independent when the survey took place, a more detailed differentiation of age cohorts would make less sense. The results of the models' estimation are presented in table 7.4.

---

[5] For example, maternity pay was paid to a woman through the institution where she worked or studied. In case if a woman was neither employed, nor enrolled in an educational institution, the maternity pay was paid to her husband at the place, where he was employed.

Table 7.4 Random-intercept Tobit regressions for age cohorts

	Model 1. Younger cohort		Model 2. Older cohort		Model 3. Both age cohorts	
	Marg. effects	*Std. Err.*	*Marg. effects*	*Std. Err.*	*Coefficient*	*Std. Err.*
Age	0.001	0.001	0.000	0.002	0.001	0.003
Female[1]	0.136***	0.025	0.124***	0.028	0.266***	0.048
Married to a working spouse[2]	0.173***	0.031	0.195***	0.034	0.332***	0.058
Single[2]	-0.056°	0.031	0.038	0.034	-0.087	0.058
Vocational education[3]	0.029	0.037	0.077°	0.040	0.068	0.068
Higher education[3]	-0.110**	0.038	0.008	0.041	-0.177**	0.063
Salesman[4]	-0.099°	0.054	-0.093	0.059	.	.
Hairdresser[4]	-0.032***	0.054	0.064	0.059	.	.
Builder[4]	-0.408**	0.054	-0.340***	0.059	.	.
Bookkeeper[4]	-0.155***	0.055	-0.117°	0.060	.	.
Doctor[4]	-0.283***	0.063	-0.272***	0.068	.	.
Journalist[4]	-0.199*	0.053	-0.184**	0.058	.	.
University professor[4]	-0.152***	0.062	-0.156*	0.068	.	.
Entrepreneur[4]	-0.314***	0.054	-0.226***	0.059	.	.
Lawyer[4]	-0.323***	0.061	-0.278***	0.068	.	.
Occupation prestige	.	.	.	.	-0.538***	0.093
Log of income before taxes	1.522***	0.012	1.527***	0.013	2.844***	0.023
One child[5]	-0.184***	0.038	-0.226***	0.042	-0.359***	0.054
Two children[5]	-0.313***	0.037	-0.304***	0.041	-0.546***	0.056
Three children[5]	-0.471***	0.038	-0.522***	0.042	-0.897***	0.062
Four children[5]	-0.615***	0.039	-0.613***	0.042	-1.109***	0.069
Average achievements[6]	-0.304***	0.031	-0.179***	0.034	-0.555***	0.058
High achievements[6]	-0.374***	0.031	-0.254***	0.034	-0.688***	0.058
Economically stable[7]	0.070*	0.031	0.020	0.034	0.143*	0.058
On the verge of bankruptcy[7]	0.178***	0.031	0.116**	0.034	0.347***	0.059
Private enterprise[8]	-0.077**	0.027	0.008	0.030	-0.148**	0.051
Older cohort of respondents[9]	.	.	.	.	-0.928**	0.337

Age*age group	.	.	.	.	-0.001	0.004
Income*age group	.	.	.	.	0.101**	0.034
Sex*age group	.	.	.	.	-0.013	0.071
Occupation*age group	.	.	.	.	0.025	0.138
Children*age group	.	.	.	.	-0.013	0.024
Private*age group	.	.	.	.	0.160*	0.076
Spouse*age group	.	.	.	.	0.043	0.088
Single*age group	.	.	.	.	0.168°	0.087
Vocational educ.*age group	.	.	.	.	0.091	0.102
Higher educ.*age group	.	.	.	.	0.182°	0.095
Average perform.*age group	.	.	.	.	0.223*	0.087
High perform.*age group	.	.	.	.	0.200*	0.087
Stable*age group	.	.	.	.	-0.104	0.087
Bankrupt*age group	.	.	.	.	-0.111	0.088
Constant	.	.	.	.	-22.856***	0.227
Respondents	985		812		1797	
Vignettes	11818		9731		21549	
Estimated random intercept standard deviation	1.209***	0.038	1.338***	0.045	1.266***	0.029
Estimated level 1 (vignettes) standard deviation	2.361***	0.021	2.433***	0.024	2.402***	0.016

° $p < 0.1$, * $p < 0.05$, ** $p < 0.01$, *** $p < 0.001$.
First two models: average marginal effects on the truncated variable, the third model: effects on the latent variable. Dependent variable is an estimation of the just income made by respondents on the 11-term scale with values from -5 (the income is too low) to 5 (the income is too high). The unit of analysis is a vignette. Reference categories: [1] Male, [2] Married to a non-working spouse, [3] Secondary education, [4] Waiter, [5] No children, [6] Low achievements, [7] High income, [8] State enterprise, [9] Younger cohort.

The judgments of the both age cohorts are very similar except for a couple of divergences. Both age cohorts regard female employees as less deserving as compared to their male counterparts. Both groups take the need criterion into consideration: the number of children is positively related to the amount of just earnings, and the availability of a second breadwinner in a family diminishes need and consequently leads to perceptions of overreward as compared to a person who is the sole breadwinner regardless of marital status. However, the younger generation has more compassion for singles and regards their incomes as unjustly too low compared to those of married people.

Contrary to the older cohort, younger people believe that the higher education of vignette persons should be reflected in a larger payment for their work. This means that the thesis of the human capital theory, which stresses the importance of investment in education for future earnings, is applied by the younger generation, but not by older citizens. Moreover, the Chow test suggests that younger cohorts ascribe more importance to the work performance of a vignette person than do older cohorts. From this, I conclude that the new generation of Ukrainians holds more pronounced meritocratic values of capitalist market societies. Only the younger generation of Ukrainians differentiates between just incomes paid in the private vs. state enterprises, ascribing higher wages to persons working in the private sector. The analysis revealed that the older cohort of Ukrainians considers, on average, lower incomes to be just. Taking into account that pensioners, who as a rule obtain lower incomes than do employed citizens, constitute over 60% of the older cohort, the expectations of lower just incomes among them match with the "is" situation.

Of particular interest for my study is the relevant weight the two generations assign to need and desert justice principles. The semi-partial R^2 values that refer to each of the vignettes' dimensions are presented in figure 7.5. These values show contribution of each of the factors to the explanation of the dependent variable (Soofi, Retzer, Yasai-Ardekani 2000, Acock 2008) and enable one to assess the relative importance of each of the factors for the justice judgments in such a way that it can be compared across models.

Figure 7.5 Justice evaluations by age cohorts

Semi-partial R^2 values associated with the vignette dimensions. The significant differences in importance assigned to the factors by the two age groups are marked by light grey color.

Older generation:

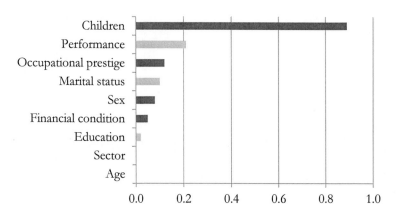

Younger generation:

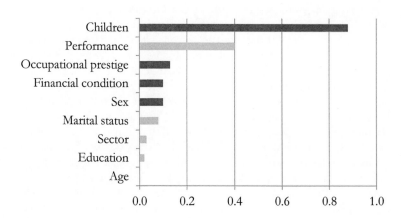

Since younger generation of Ukrainians places more weight on desert-related characteristics such as higher education and work performance as compared to older people, the data provide support to the assumption derived from the socialization theory. Nevertheless, the effect of the number of children in a family exceeds substantially all other effects in the model and is identical for both groups. In other words, the need principle receives the same, considerable support among younger and older citizens. This finding points to the domination of the need justice principle in the respondents' judgments irrespective of age. Thus, the ideological socialization thesis, stating that people who were less socialized in the Soviet Union would support the need principle less, is rejected by the empirical results. This implies that support for the need principle cannot be explained simply by ascribing its origins to the communist ideology. A more plausible explanation is that the high level of support of the need principle is caused by the low level of incomes considered (incomes that do not suffice to ensure a descent life standard under conditions of the weak social security system). This explanation was discussed in the section 7.6 and it states that the strong support of the need principle relates to the struggle of people for the social minimum.

7.7.2 How does level of education shape people's views on what is just?

According to the human capital and labor market theories, educational attainment is one of the major predictors of income in a market economy. As the previous analysis has shown, Ukrainians mainly ignore the educational attainment of the vignette persons when they judge the justice of incomes. However, according to rational choice theory, this behavior is rational only for those who do not possess an appropriately high level of education. Individuals who have invested more in acquisition of special professional knowledge are likely to expect higher reward for their work, which is deemed to be associated with higher productivity. In other words, it is plausible to expect that there is a difference in justice judgments between those who have better education and those who are less educated.

I hypothesize that the individuals with higher or vocational education would expect higher rewards for the better educated vignette persons than would respondents with secondary general education, primary education or less. Testing this assumption implies running regressions for these two educational groups and exploring the differences in the weight ascribed to each of the factors. The results of the random-intercept Tobit regressions for the two educational groups are presented in table 7.5.

Table 7.5 Random-intercept Tobit regressions for educational groups

	Model 1. Primary/secondary		Model 2. Vocational/higher		Model 3. Both groups	
	Marg. effects	Std. Err.	Marg. effects	Std. Err.	Coefficient	Std. Err.
Age	0.001	0.001	0.000	0.002	0.002	0.003
Female[1]	0.149***	0.024	0.107***	0.030	0.295***	0.045
Married to a working spouse[2]	0.186***	0.029	0.184***	0.036	0.360***	0.056
Single[2]	0.001	0.029	-0.025	0.036	0.020	0.056
Vocational education[3]	0.063°	0.035	0.030	0.043	0.130*	0.065
Higher education[3]	-0.034	0.036	-0.088*	0.044	-0.053	0.061
Salesman[4]	-0.090°	0.052	-0.099	0.064	.	.
Hairdresser[4]	0.020	0.052	0.005	0.064	.	.
Builder[4]	-0.344***	0.052	-0.422***	0.063	.	.
Bookkeeper[4]	-0.124*	0.052	-0.158*	0.065	.	.
Doctor[4]	-0.280***	0.060	-0.277***	0.073	.	.
Journalist[4]	-0.198***	0.051	-0.182**	0.062	.	.
University professor[4]	-0.126*	0.059	-0.187*	0.072	.	.
Entrepreneur[4]	-0.199***	0.052	-0.384***	0.063	.	.
Lawyer[4]	-0.202**	0.058	-0.462***	0.072	.	.
Occupation prestige	.	.	.	.	-0.400***	0.089
Log of income before taxes	1.521***	0.011	1.535***	0.014	2.877***	0.022
One child[5]	-0.228***	0.036	-0.161***	0.045	-0.375***	0.054
Two children[5]	-0.305***	0.035	-0.311***	0.044	-0.582***	0.056
Three children[5]	-0.506***	0.036	-0.470***	0.045	-0.948***	0.061
Four children[5]	-0.648***	0.037	-0.558***	0.045	-1.182***	0.066
Average achievements[6]	-0.217***	0.029	-0.292***	0.036	-0.396***	0.055
High achievements[6]	-0.260***	0.029	-0.409***	0.036	-0.486***	0.056
Economically stable[7]	0.043	0.029	0.057	0.036	0.087	0.056
On the verge of bankruptcy[7]	0.132***	0.030	0.180***	0.037	0.267***	0.056
Private enterprise[8]	0.006	0.026	-0.108**	0.032	0.007	0.048
Resp. with better education[9]	.	.	.	.	0.091	0.343

Age*educ. group	.	.	.	.	-0.003	0.004
Income*educ. group	.	.	.	.	0.035	0.035
Sex* educ. group	.	.	.	.	-0.083	0.072
Occupation*educ. group	.	.	.	.	-0.329*	0.141
Children*educ. Group	.	.	.	.	0.032	0.025
Private*educ. Group	.	.	.	.	-0.210**	0.077
Spouse*educ. Group	.	.	.	.	-0.013	0.089
Single*educ. Group	.	.	.	.	-0.067	0.089
Vocational educ.*educ. group	.	.	.	.	-0.058	0.103
Higher educ.*educ. Group	.	.	.	.	-0.103	0.097
Average perform.*educ. group	.	.	.	.	-0.149°	0.088
High perform.*educ. group	.	.	.	.	-0.280**	0.089
Stable*educ. Group	.	.	.	.	0.025	0.089
Bankrupt*educ. Group	.	.	.	.	0.077	0.090
Constant	.	.	.	.	-23.346***	0.218
Respondents	1087		707		1794	
Vignettes	13 037		8 476		21513	
Estimated random intercept std. dev.	1.278***	0.038	1.246***	0.046	1.264***	0.029
Estimated level 1 (vignettes) std. dev.	2.399***	0.020	2.387***	0.025	2.403***	0.016

° p < 0.1, * p < 0.05, ** p < 0.01, *** p < 0.001

First two models: average marginal effects on the truncated variable, the third model: effects on the latent variable. Dependent variable is an estimation of the just income made by respondents on the 11-term scale with values from -5 (the income is too low) to 5 (the income is too high). The unit of analysis is a vignette. Reference categories: [1] Male, [2] Married to a non-working spouse, [3] Secondary education, [4] Waiter, [5] No children, [6] Low achievements, [7] High income, [8] State enterprise, [9] Respondents without higher or vocational education.

The results presented in the table 7.5 indicate that the vignette subjects with higher education were perceived by better educated respondents as deserving higher earnings as compared to fictitious persons with only general secondary education. The corresponding negative coefficient referring to the group of less educated respondents is not significant.

Although this outcome was expected according to my assumption, the Chow test does not reveal significant difference between judgments of both groups of citizens with respect to the meaning of the educational attainment for determination of just earnings. This implies that the difference in judgments of the two educational groups is not sufficiently pronounced. That is, Ukrainian citizens do not place a lot of weight on the formal educational attainment when defining just wages. As mentioned above, this result is likely to reflect people's perception of a weak relationship between official diplomas and actual qualifications and skills.

On the other hand, the analysis revealed a significant difference with respect to the vignette dimension, which was defined as a more appropriate measure of human capital than was formal educational attainment.

The analysis has shown that the better educated groups of the population place more weight on the prestige of occupations and high work performance of an employee (figure 7.6). The ascription of higher value to this desert-related factor by better educated respondents provides support for the rational choice statement, which argues that those with better education would advocate for higher rewards for those who have made larger investments in their human capital.

As in previous models, the dimension of one's work performance has the strongest effect on the amount of just earnings among other desert-related characteristics. At the same time, need considerations preserve their first-rate position in the ordering of factors.

Respondents with less education make no distinction between private or state enterprises, while better-educated respondents believe that employees in the private sector should earn more than those employed in the state sector. The gender-discriminating attitude remains equally evident in both educational groups; irrespective of their level of education, respondents reproduce the gender wage gap in their distributive justice judgments.

Figure 7.6 Justice evaluations by educational groups

Semi-partial R^2 values associated with the vignette dimensions. The significant differences in importance assigned to the factors by the two age groups are marked by light grey color.

Primary and secondary education

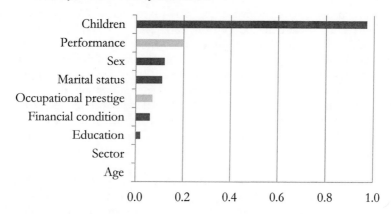

Vocational and higher education

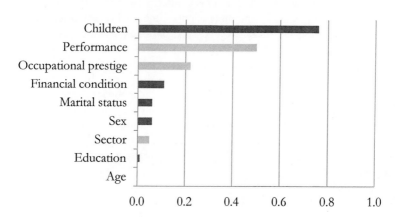

7.7.3 The effect of region and locality type on justice perception

As regional perspectives contribute to the explanation of many differences in various attitudes of Ukrainians, I explore the extent of agreement in distributive justice attitudes in the two most contrasting regions of Ukraine. For this reason, I omit the central and southern regions from further analysis and focus my attention exclusively on the eastern and western regions as defined in table 5.2.

The adaptation and cognitive dissonance theory postulate that people adjust their expectations to their definition of the actual situation while judging it from their immediate social environment. I assume, therefore, that respondents coming from the more industrially developed eastern region would generally expect higher just earnings than would those residing in the western region of Ukraine.

The results of the random-intercept Tobit regressions are presented in table 7.6. The test of the hypothesis revealed that people from the western part of Ukraine indeed assess lower wages to be just as compared to the wages perceived to be just by the population of the eastern region.

The distributive justice judgments of people from both regions of Ukraine are generally marked by a high degree of similarity. The analysis uncovered two further differences in the justice judgments of these two population groups (figure 7.7).

First, the effect of high work performance is more important for the residents of the eastern Ukraine. Second, the effect of the vocational education on the justice judgments of people from the western part of the country is significant but is not in the direction predicted by the human capital theory. Since none of the middle range theories considered in this study provides any valid explanation of this relationship, the interpretation of this result is reserved for future research.

Table 7.6 Random-intercept Tobit regressions for western and eastern Ukraine

	Model 1. Western Ukraine		Model 2. Eastern Ukraine		Model 3. Both regions	
	Marg. effects	*Std. Err.*	*Marg. effects*	*Std. Err.*	*Coefficient*	*Std. Err.*
Age	0.003	0.002	0.000	0.002	0.005	0.004
Female[1]	0.043	0.042	0.120**	0.039	0.091	0.076
Married to a working spouse[2]	0.241***	0.052	0.169***	0.047	0.459***	0.094
Single[2]	-0.011	0.051	-0.007	0.047	-0.001	0.093
Vocational education[3]	0.152*	0.062	0.022	0.057	0.316**	0.109
Higher education[3]	-0.027	0.063	-0.084	0.058	0.024	0.102
Salesman[4]	-0.112	0.091	-0.082	0.083	.	.
Hairdresser[4]	-0.078	0.091	0.080	0.083	.	.
Builder[4]	-0.384***	0.091	-0.380***	0.083	.	.
Bookkeeper[4]	-0.172o	0.092	-0.169*	0.084	.	.
Doctor[4]	-0.291**	0.105	-0.279**	0.096	.	.
Journalist[4]	-0.363***	0.089	-0.259**	0.082	.	.
University professor[4]	-0.205*	0.104	-0.208*	0.095	.	.
Entrepreneur[4]	-0.236**	0.090	-0.365***	0.083	.	.
Lawyer[4]	-0.168	0.103	-0.355***	0.095	.	.
Occupation prestige	.	.	.	.	-0.466**	0.149
Log of income before taxes	1.490***	0.018	1.507***	0.019	2.757***	0.037
One child[5]	-0.246***	0.063	-0.133*	0.058	-0.314***	0.084
Two children [5]	-0.437***	0.062	-0.271***	0.057	-0.579***	0.088
Three children [5]	-0.560***	0.063	-0.593***	0.059	-0.983***	0.098
Four children [5]	-0.637***	0.064	-0.771***	0.059	-1.191***	0.110
Average achievements[6]	-0.261***	0.052	-0.211***	0.047	-0.457***	0.093
High achievements[6]	-0.252***	0.052	-0.357***	0.047	-0.449***	0.093
Economically stable[7]	0.065	0.051	0.077	0.047	0.128	0.093
On the verge of bankruptcy[7]	0.161**	0.052	0.200***	0.048	0.315**	0.095
Private enterprise[8]	-0.047	0.045	-0.023	0.041	-0.096	0.081
East[9]	.	.	.	.	-0.883o	0.510
Age*region	.	.	.	.	-0.006	0.006
Income*region	.	.	.	.	0.146**	0.052
Sex*region	.	.	.	.	0.144	0.108

Occupation*region	.	.	.	.	-0.331	0.211
Children*region	.	.	.	.	-0.059	0.037
Private*region	.	.	.	.	0.048	0.115
Spouse*region	.	.	.	.	-0.130	0.133
Single*region	.	.	.	.	0.003	0.132
Vocational education*region	.	.	.	.	-0.267°	0.154
Higher education*region	.	.	.	.	-0.143	0.144
Average performance*region	.	.	.	.	0.046	0.132
High performance*region	.	.	.	.	-0.231°	0.132
Stable*region	.	.	.	.	0.020	0.132
Bankrupt*region	.	.	.	.	0.088	0.134
Constant	.	.	.	.	-22.384***	0.362
Respondents	398		391		789	
Vignettes	4772		4691		9463	
Estimated random intercept standard deviation	1.376***	0.065	1.049***	0.059	1.222***	0.044
Estimated level 1 (vignettes) standard deviation	2.357***	0.033	2.505***	0.035	2.443***	0.024

$^{\circ}$ p<0.1, * p < 0.05, ** p < 0.01, *** p < 0.001.
First two models: average marginal effects on the truncated variable, the third model: effects on the latent variable. Dependent variable is an estimation of the just income made by respondents on the 11-term scale with values from -5 (the income is too low) to 5 (the income is too high). The unit of analysis is a vignette. Reference categories: [1] Male, [2] Married to a non-working spouse, [3] Secondary education, [4] Waiter, [5] No children, [6] Low achievements, [7] High income, [8] State enterprise, [9] West.

Apart from disparities between the regions, there are noticeable differences within them. Post-Soviet states are generally characterized by large inequalities between urban and rural areas. The villages generally provide much poorer standards of living, worse quality of facilities and underdeveloped infrastructure for their inhabitants as compared to large urban centers. Since poverty became an increasingly rural phenomenon in Ukraine and because people usually take the immediate social environment as a reference point for their own attitudes, I assumed that the respondents residing in the villages and small towns would expect generally lower just wages than would city dwellers.

Figure 7.7 Justice evaluations by region

Semi-partial R^2 values associated with the vignette dimensions. The significant differences in importance assigned to the factors by the two age groups are marked by light grey color.

Eastern Ukraine

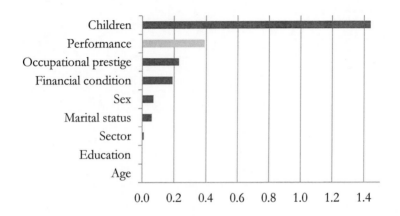

Western Ukraine

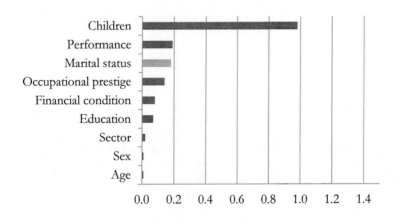

Table 7.7 Random-intercept Tobit regressions for urban and rural population

	Model 1. Urban		Model 2. Rural		Model 3. Both	
	Marg. effects	Std Err	Marg. effects	Std Err	Coefficient	Std Err
Age	0.000	0.001	0.001	0.002	0.002	0.003
Female[1]	0.153***	0.023	0.093**	0.032	0.181**	0.060
Married to a working spouse[2]	0.184***	0.028	0.186***	0.039	0.351***	0.074
Single[2]	-0.019	0.028	0.008	0.039	0.024	0.073
Vocational education[3]	0.042	0.034	0.072	0.047	0.132	0.086
Higher education[3]	-0.068*	0.034	-0.027	0.048	-0.060	0.080
Salesman[4]	-0.121**	0.049	-0.036	0.069	.	.
Hairdresser[4]	0.017	0.049	0.011	0.069	.	.
Builder[4]	-0.462***	0.049	-0.209**	0.068	.	.
Bookkeeper[4]	-0.150**	0.050	-0.110	0.070	.	.
Doctor[4]	-0.325***	0.057	-0.194*	0.079	.	.
Journalist[4]	-0.242***	0.048	-0.101	0.067	.	.
University professor[4]	-0.182**	0.056	-0.089	0.078	.	.
Entrepreneur[4]	-0.317***	0.049	-0.185**	0.069	.	.
Lawyer[4]	-0.348***	0.056	-0.212**	0.077	.	.
Occupational prestige	.	.	.	.	-0.374**	0.117
Log of income before taxes	1.509***	0.011	1.556***	0.014	2.907***	0.029
One child[5]	-0.210***	0.035	-0.186***	0.048	-0.360***	0.056
Two children[5]	-0.283***	0.034	-0.353***	0.047	-0.548***	0.062
Three children[5]	-0.495***	0.035	-0.488***	0.048	-0.902***	0.072
Four children[5]	-0.619***	0.035	-0.597***	0.049	-1.118***	0.085
Average achievements[6]	-0.251***	0.028	-0.238***	0.039	-0.434***	0.073
High achievements[6]	-0.350***	0.028	-0.263***	0.039	-0.481***	0.073
Economically stable[7]	0.058*	0.028	0.027	0.039	0.055	0.073
On the verge of bankruptcy[7]	0.151***	0.028	0.150***	0.039	0.287***	0.074
Private enterprise[8]	-0.032	0.024	-0.053	0.034	-0.090	0.064
Urban[9]	.	.	.	.	0.188	0.352
Age*urban	.	.	.	.	-0.002	0.004
Income*urban	.	.	.	.	-0.028	0.036
Sex*urban	.	.	.	.	0.123°	0.074
Occupation*urban	.	.	.	.	-0.241°	0.145
Children*urban	.	.	.	.	-0.005	0.025
Private*urban	.	.	.	.	0.018	0.079
Spouse*urban	.	.	.	.	0.005	0.091

Chapter Seven

Single*urban	.	.	.	.	-0.046	0.091
Vocational education*urban	.	.	.	.	-0.034	0.106
Higher education*urban	.	.	.	.	-0.048	0.099
Average performance*urban	.	.	.	.	-0.033	0.090
High performance*urban	.	.	.	.	-0.179*	0.091
Stable*urban	.	.	.	.	0.063	0.091
Bankrupt*urban	.	.	.	.	0.015	0.092
Constant	.	.	.	.	-23.402***	0.285
Respondents	659		1138		1797	
Vignettes	7901		13648		21549	
Estimated random intercept standard deviation	1.303***	0.049	1.244***	0.036	1.265***	0.029
Estimated level 1 (vignettes) standard deviation	2.464***	0.026	2.348***	0.019	2.403***	0.016

° $p<0.1$, * $p < 0.05$, ** $p < 0.01$, *** $p < 0.001$
First two models: average marginal effects on the truncated variable, the third model: effects on the latent variable. Dependent variable is an estimation of the just income made by respondents on the 11-term scale with values from -5 (the income is too low) to 5 (the income is too high). The unit of analysis is a vignette. Reference categories: [1] Male, [2] Married to a non-working spouse, [3] Secondary education, [4] Waiter, [5] No children, [6] Low achievements, [7] High income, [8] State enterprise, [9] Rural.

Because the capital city of Ukraine, Kyiv, and other large cities of the country are important economic, political and cultural centers, they attract the most qualified labor force from the regions and offer the highest quality of life in the country. That is, urban centers accumulate greater human capital as compared to rural areas. Bearing this in mind, I hypothesized that dwellers of the urban centers would place more value on desert-related characteristics. A second hypothesis is that the urban population, enjoying better living conditions and better-paid jobs, would assess higher earnings' amounts as just on average. The results of the regressions for the urban and rural population are presented in table 7.7.

Figure 7.8 Justice evaluations by locality type

Semi-partial R^2 values associated with the vignette dimensions. The significant differences in importance assigned to the factors by the two age groups are marked by light grey color.

Urban population

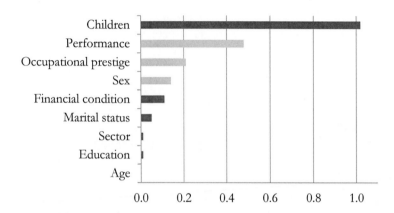

Rural population

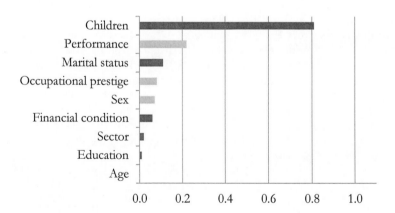

The group of urban dwellers comprises those residing in the cities with a population over 250,000 inhabitants including the capital city, while the rural population includes those living in the small towns (up to 250,000 people) and villages.

The analysis of the interaction terms (model 3, table 7.7) revealed the differences in perception of the role of work performance, occupational prestige and sex of a vignette person for the definition of her just wages. In line with the rational choice statement, urban population characterized by a higher human capital ascribes greater importance to the factors of high work performance and occupational prestige.

The second assumption about larger just incomes in the big cities compared to small towns and villages found insufficient empirical support (the interaction term is not significant at the conventional level). Unexpectedly, the urban population appears to be more discriminant against female fictitious persons with respect to the level of labor remuneration. Although the effect of the female dummy is significant in both population groups, it is weaker among the Ukrainian respondents coming from rural areas. Further research is needed to clarify the reasons for this difference in justice attitudes between urban and rural population groups.

A more detailed look at the response patterns clarifies that the most distinct difference between expectations of just earnings are apparent not between the urban and rural population but between the residents of Kyiv and the rest of Ukraine (figure 7.9). The capital city dwellers consider much higher incomes to be just compared to the rest of respondents. The income values of 400, 600, and 800 UAH are uniformly considered as extremely low by the respondents from Kyiv. Moreover, contrary to the rest of the population, wages of 4000 UAH are considered by the capital city dwellers as rather unjustly too low. The justice attitudes of respondents reflect the actual inequalities between the capital city and the rest of the country (e.g., Pracja Ukrajiny u 2009 roci: 191). This finding again demonstrates the high degree of correspondence between the real situation and people's justice attitudes.

Figure 7.9 Evaluations of vignette incomes depending on place of residence, mean values

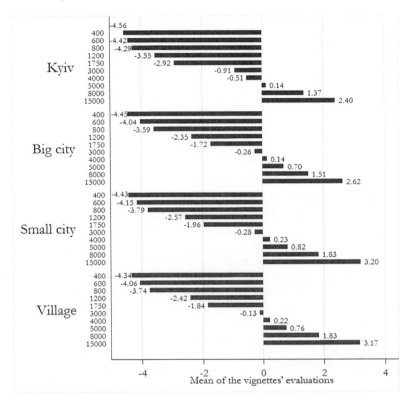

7.8 The just wages

In this section, I complement my empirical analysis by turning the focus from the relative importance of justice principles in justice judgments of respondents to the absolute values of earnings considered just by them.

In order to compute the just wages in the absolute terms, I use the approach of G. Jasso (2007) with modifications presented by K. Auspurg and A. Jäckle (2012).

Accordingly, the amount of just earnings in national currency (UAH) is computed using the following equation:

$$justinc_j = inc_j \cdot exp(-E(J_j) \,/\, \beta_{inc}),$$

where inc_j is a value of income dimension in vignette j, $E(J_j)$ – expected judgment on the vignette j, and β_{inc} – regression coefficient related to the income dimension.

According to respondents' judgments, a mean just income in Ukraine is assessed as 3949 UAH[6]. This sum is more than two times higher than the actual official average monthly wage given by the State Statistics Service of Ukraine in 2009 – 1906 UAH[7]. This fact stresses that people's expectations towards just earnings are in conflict with the actual state of affairs.

According to the theoretically grounded assumptions presented in section 5.3, two types of factors have an impact on the amount of just earnings: the information presented in the vignettes as well as the social-demographic profile of those expressing the justice judgments. The following paragraphs address the computation of the just wages in absolute terms for each of the cases defined by the diversity of vignette and person's characteristics. The computations of the just wages are based on the multilevel Tobit regression (presented in table 7.6).

7.8.1 The relevance of vignette's characteristics

Table 7.8 displays the average just wages for different fictitious persons. Only those vignette characteristics that were significant in the initial model are treated (table 7.2, model 2).

Holding all other effects constant, male employees deserve, according to people's judgments, about 10% higher wages than do women. Further, respondents believe that individuals married to a working spouse should earn about 300-500 UAH less than those married to a non-working spouse or single. Employees with no children should on average earn 1644 UAH less than should those who have four children in their family.

---

[6] This and further assessments of just wages are based on the fitted values of the random-intercept Tobit model for laten variable (described in section 7.2).
[7] Source: Pracja Ukrajiny u 2009 roci (2010: 209).

Table 7.8 Average just wages by vignette person's characteristics

	Average just wages (UAH)	N of vignettes
Male	4159	10597
Female	3746	10967
Married, non-working spouse	4128	7453
Married, working spouse	3610	6826
Single	4084	7285
Waiter	3450	2434
Salesman	3615	2242
Hairdresser	3453	2165
Builder	4375	2330
Bookkeeper	3791	2253
Doctor	4394	1701
Journalist	3945	2515
University professor	4180	1794
Entrepreneur	4121	2336
Lawyer	4419	1794
Person having no children	3266	7102
Person having 1 child	3778	3593
Person having 2 children	3907	3679
Person having 3 children	4552	3600
Person having 4 children	4910	3590
Person with low performance	3464	7192
Person with average performance	4041	7177
Person with high performance	4342	7195
Private enterprise	4013	14395
State enterprise	3821	7169
Organization on the verge of bankruptcy	3722	7002
Economically stable organization	4011	7447
Organization making high revenues	4109	7115

There is no consecutive order in the amounts of just earnings ascribed to occupations if scale of occupational prestige is taken as the reference ordering. It is also remarkable that the range of just earnings for the considered occupations is relatively narrow. These two peculiarities suggest that according to people's perceptions, the dimension of occupational prestige is not the defining key factor of the just social stratification in modern Ukraine. People believe that waiters, hairdressers, journalists and bookkeepers should earn nearly the same wages[8] although the prestige related to these professions is different. The amount of just wages ascribed to a builder is almost the same as that defined as just for a university professor. This finding, on the one hand, is reminiscent of Soviet times: "In former communist countries, education has not been valued as highly in terms of higher earnings. Typically doctors and professors and others with higher education did not get much more than the average worker" (Aalberg 2003: 58). On the other hand, the just amounts of earnings derived from the vignettes relate only to official wages and do not account for the widespread additional, extra and informal payments.

A distinct effect of the work performance is reflected in respondents' ascribing of about 878 UAH more to persons having higher performance as compared to those who have low performance at work. Private enterprises are expected to pay about 200 UAH higher wages to employees as compared to the state organizations, while people are less adverse to receiving lower pay from enterprises facing insolvency, even if they pay almost 400 UAH less than organizations receiving high revenues.

7.8.2 The relevance of respondent's characteristics

The average just earnings depending on the characteristics of people who express the distributive justice judgments are shown in the table 7.9.

According to the data, respondents living in the central and eastern regions believe higher wages to be just compared to those residing in the southern and western part of the country. Similarly, the urban population regards higher earnings as just compared to rural population. Men and women judge almost the same amounts of earnings to be just. Better-educated respondents generally expect slightly higher wages than respondents with only secondary education or less. The group of

---

[8] This conclusion may be drawn if the possible distorting effect of the respondents' consideration of the possibility of informal additional payments is not taken into account.

respondents aged over 60 years defines somewhat lower wages to be just compared to those between the ages of 18 and 60 years old. Those over 60 years of age are nearly all pensioners, who, as a rule, are more affected by poverty in Ukraine. Therefore, this finding is entirely in line with the assumption of the shaping effect of reality on justice attitudes, which reflects the consequences of adaptation and cognitive dissonance reduction mechanisms.

Table 7.9 Average just wages by respondent's characteristics

Respondent's characteristics	Average just wages (UAH)	N of vignettes
Region: West	3839	4692
Region: Center	4056	6312
Region: South	3794	5784
Region: East	4165	4776
Urban population	4229	7908
Rural population	3806	13656
Male	3977	9720
Female	3929	11844
Higher/vocational education	4017	8484
Secondary/primary education and less	3905	13044
Aged 18-30	4041	4812
Aged 31-60	4033	12288
Aged 60 and above	3667	4452

The just gender wage gap seems to be wider in the eastern part of Ukraine than in the western part (figure 7.10). Respondents from the eastern region ascribe 4524 UAH as an average just wage to a male vignette person and only 4086 UAH to a female, while those living in the western region assess these amounts respectively as 3920 and 3751 UAH.

Figure 7.10 Just earnings by gender, answers of respondents from two regions, mean values

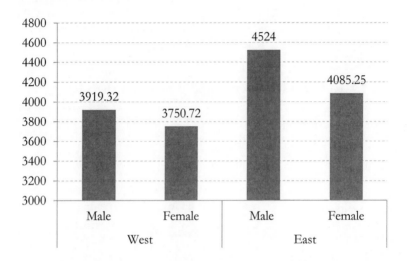

CHAPTER EIGHT

COMPARATIVE PERSPECTIVE: JUSTICE ATTITUDES IN UKRAINE AND GERMANY

The empirical results presented in the previous chapter suggest that social environment has an enormous shaping effect on justice judgments. To enhance the reliability of this statement, I explore parallels between reality and people's justice attitudes from a comparative perspective. A comparison of people's justice attitudes across different countries could be very informative in many respects. It allows not only for deeper insight into the actual social mechanisms that explain the role of social structures in shaping justice attitudes and for refinement of the general picture of distributive justice attitudes, but also allows for the detection of similarities and the assessment of the universality of justice principles across different cultures and institutional contexts.

Germany, being among the most successful democracies of the European Union, serves in this study as a reference society. A comparison of fundamental justice views between Ukraine and Germany provides an opportunity to reveal the extent to which attitudes of people differ and the reason behind this difference. Investigating the disparities in distributive justice attitudes of Ukrainians and Germans implies, among others, taking the major saliences of the income distribution and redistribution systems currently existing in these two countries into account.

With respect to empirical justice research, German sociologists have scientifically contributed to many aspects of the field including the development of the factorial survey methods for studying justice attitudes (see Auspurg, Hinz, Liebig 2009, Sauer et al. 2011). In recent years, German sociologists explored different methodological issues and elaborated practical recommendations regarding numerous important details such as optimal number of vignettes to be assessed by the respondents, the effect of implausible descriptions on the respondents' reactions reflected in their response behavior, and the capacities of the different respondent groups to evaluate the vignettes of different levels of complexity. The findings of German social scientists are of paramount value to the further development of this method as well as to the practical usage of factorial designs in large-scale population surveys. In 2008, the factorial survey design was implemented in a representative population survey in Germany – Socio-Economic Panel Pretest survey (SOEP-Pretest 2008). The factorial survey module treated the topic of distributive justice attitudes. The availability of the SOEP-Pretest 2008 dataset was advantageous for the following analysis since both of the surveys used practically the same design of the vignette module, allowing for valuable and novel conclusions on the research issue at hand.

Because my study considers theoretical statements that can be better verified by empirical evidence drawn from a cross-national comparative study, the availability of the appropriate dataset provided additional motivation to compare Ukraine with Germany.

At the same time, it is common for there to be significant restrictions in the research design of cross-national studies. The principal restriction deals with the fact that the questions used in the questionnaire are thought to be meaningful and relevant to all participating countries and therefore abstract from specific country features that may be important for a deep analysis. Other constraining factors for the elaboration of the research design of a cross-national comparative study originate from different availability and coverage of sampling frames, unequal abilities of survey research organizations to conduct fieldwork, cultural and language peculiarities, etc. Ukraine and Germany have different survey traditions and practices. The task of the researcher is to develop the optimal research design that would be general enough to be applied in both countries but also sufficiently specific in order to get the most precise information on the research problem. Because of the different social contexts in Ukraine and Germany, some of the vignette dimensions or values diverge (see chapter 6 above), which ensures the absence of irrelevant or meaningless situation descriptions in the questionnaire.

In the following section, I introduce the SOEP-Pretest 2008 survey data and its vignette module. Furthermore, I proceed with the test of the assumption that there is a shaping effect of the actual distributive practices on the justice attitudes of people in Ukraine and Germany and compare the degree of correspondence between actual wages and wages perceived as just in absolute terms. Finally, I compare empirical results from the analysis of the factorial survey with classic attitudes measurement module coming from ISSP 2009.

8.1 SOEP-Pretest 2008

Sauer et al. (2009a, 2009b) describe the major findings of the distributive justice module of the SOEP-Pretest 2008 for the western and eastern Germany. The survey was conducted in the form of computer assisted personal interviews (CAPI) in August 2008. In total, 1066 people of the German population ages 16 or older participated in the survey. For the following analysis, only 944 respondents who were born before the transformation (1989) and have not lived abroad (80% residents of West Germany and 20% residents of East Germany) are considered. The factorial survey module of the questionnaire included 24 vignettes. In total, 240 different vignettes were used. One of ten different questionnaire versions (decks) was randomly assigned to each respondent (Sauer et al 2009a, 2009b).

Table 8.1. Vignette dimensions and their levels, SOEP-Pretest 2008

Dimension	Levels
Age	25, 35, 45, 55 years
Sex	Male, female
Marital status	Single earner, married, double earner, married, single
Vocational training	With, without vocational training, with university degree
Occupation*	Manufacturing laborer, doorman, locomotive engine driver, administrative associate professional, hairdresser, social work professional, computer programmer, electrical engineer, general manager, medical doctor
Gross income (in EUR)**	500, 950, 1200, 1500, 2500, 3800, 5400, 6800, 10000, 15000
Children	No child, 1 child, 2 children, 3 children, 4 children
Performance on the job	Below, above average, average
Economic situation of the company	High profit, economical solid, threatened by bankruptcy
Company size	Small, medium, large

* For regression analyses: transformed into prestige values on a Magnitude Prestige Scale.
** The categories are related to the percentiles of the income distribution of fulltime employees 2007 in Germany (data source: SOEP 2007). The highest and lowest categories are added to have extreme cases.

In order to collect the evaluation of the just earnings, the SOEP-Pretest vignette module used a special 3-stage answer technique. In the first stage, the respondent had to assess the earnings amount of a vignette person as either fair or not fair. In the case of "fair" income rating, the next vignette from a respective deck was proposed to the respondent. When an "unfair" estimate was obtained, the respondent was asked to specify whether the income was too high or too low. Finally, in the third stage, the respondent had to assess the degree of injustice by a free choice of any value on the scale from 1 to 100. Although the 3-stage answer technique was rather successfully applied in the SOEP-Pretest study, methodological findings demonstrate that the standard ordinal scale is much better perceived by the respondents and causes less confusion in its application. Table 8.1 presents the vignette dimensions and values used in the SOEP-Pretest survey[1]

8.2 Country specific perceptions of income justice

In comparison to the incompatible results published by other surveys on justice attitudes, the advantage of the SOEP-Pretest dataset for the present analysis is that not only societies in general but also groups of respondents within the societies can be directly compared with each other. Since by the time of publishing of the present book, a scientific paper on this issue was published (Auspurg, Gatskova, Hinz 2013) in which I presented the major part of the comparative analysis results in collaboration with T. Hinz and K. Auspurg, I will further rely on this publication to highlight the main findings.

Figure 8.1 displays the semi-partial R-square values associated with the vignette dimensions in East and West Germany[2] and in Ukraine. The ordering of the predictors point to the overall domination of the merit justice principles in Germany contrary to Ukraine, where the principle of need is by far the most significant.

Out of all vignette dimensions used, occupational prestige carries the highest importance for defining just wages in Germany (Auspurg, Gatskova, Hinz 2013). Work performance and education are the next most relevant determinants of just wages. This means that the first three positions in the ordering of factors affecting justice attitudes of people in both parts of the country are the desert-related characteristics.

---

[1] The dimensions are practically identical to those used in the Ukrainian study (table 6.1).
[2] This distinction is drawn because western Germany is considered to be a developed capitalist democracy, while eastern Germany may still be seen as a transition society.

Figure 8.1. Distributive practices perceived as just in Ukraine and Germany

Western Germany

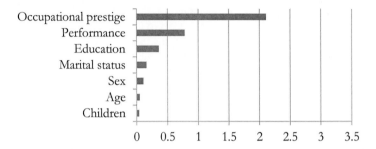

Eastern Germany

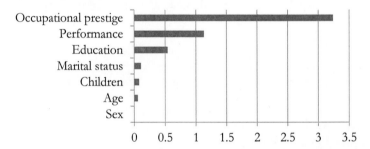

Ukraine

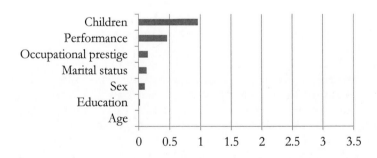

Source: Auspurg, Gatskova, Hinz (2013: 82).

The effect of the children dimension in Germany occupies a relatively low position in the general ordering of factors.

The Ukrainian case provides a different pattern of judgments marked by the dominance of the need principle. The strongest impact among vignette characteristics was attributed to the number of children. This finding is in line with my hypothesis stating that the need justice principle would dominate in the aggregated justice judgments of Ukrainian respondents due to the prevalence of objectively low earnings in Ukrainian society and in the vignettes.

The comparison of justice attitudes among educational and age groups within Germany and Ukraine uncovered several differences. According to K. Auspurg, K. Gatskova and T. Hinz (2013), the older generation in western Germany ascribes slightly higher weight to the gender of a rewardee relative to the younger generation. At the same time, occupational prestige, work performance and education are the three most important characteristics that define the amounts of just wages among all age and educational groups in the western and eastern Germany. The need considerations play a relatively negligent role as to compared with the desert-related characteristics. The socialization hypothesis finds some support in the observation that the younger cohort of German respondents ascribes more importance to work performance as compared to older people. The rational choice thesis is supported by the findings from western and eastern Germany because in both regions, better-educated respondents are more motivated by the desert-related characteristics as compared to less educated individuals.

Overall, the justice judgments of Ukrainian respondents appear to be less consistent as compared to the judgments of German citizens. There is a large degree of volatility that makes people judge the justice of incomes as if they have no clear understanding of distributive norms. However, there is an enormous consensus across population groups as to the application of the need principle, which is likely to reflect the wish of people to ensure a decent standard of living for all citizens. The revealed inconsistency of justice judgments, however, conforms to the findings of comparative studies showing that income equality is judged more inconsistently in the transformation societies as compared to Western democracies (Wegener, Liebig 1995, Wegener, Steinmann 1995). Scholars discuss the possible causes of this inconsistency in the justice attitudes and argue that it may be the clash of old and new socialization patterns (Mason 1995) or a shaping effect of reality: if the applied labor remuneration principles are unclear, people may be confused and indecisive about justice principles that should operate in society (Kluegel, Mason, Wegener 1995).

These findings suggest that the social mechanisms of the formation of justice attitudes are generally the same for the people from different countries. The resulting attitudes may, however, differ considerably. This is likely to happen mostly because of the different institutional contexts of the societies. The data suggest that the social environment is taken as a reference point by respondents for the formation of attitudes, and it thus has a substantial effect on people's justice perceptions. In a relatively stable environment, people are likely to adapt to the existing rules of the wealth distribution and to adjust their expectations to them. In a changing social system, the orientations of people become more uncertain. Irrespective of social context, the universal mechanisms that provide a valid explanation for the divergences in actual justice attitudes across population groups relate to the rational choice, socialization, human capital and labor market theories.

8.3 Actual and just earnings in Ukraine and Germany

In order to look closer at the parallels between reality and the justice judgments of people, I compute the average just wages for different occupations in the two countries and compare these values to the official statistics.

Table 8.2 enumerates the actual monthly earnings and monthly earnings considered just in Ukraine and Germany. The just wages in Germany are based on the assessment of an OLS regression model with robust standard errors, while for the case of Ukraine, the multilevel Tobit model.

The figures reveal a high level of correspondence between people's views on fair incomes by occupational groups and a hierarchy of occupations (measured on the scale of occupational prestige) in Germany. This implies the prevalence of the same point of reference for people's justice judgments. The answer patterns of German respondents suggest that there is an established understanding of occupational hierarchy on the labor market and that people reproduce it in their evaluations of just earnings. A comparison between actual and just monthly wages reveals few inconsistencies between scale of occupational prestige and the actual ordering of earnings by occupational groups. For instance, the actual wage of a hairdresser (1305 EUR) is much lower than the just income ascribed to this occupation (2367 EUR). In general, the ranking of just wages more or less reflects the ordering on the scale of occupational prestige.

I assumed that complex changes associated with the transformation process in Ukraine would affect the system of orientations of citizens and that they would be reflected in their justice judgments. In line with this assumption and contrary to German results, the assessments of just earnings in Ukraine do not correspond to the national scale of occupational prestige. This allows me to conclude that either Ukrainian respondents have no homogeneous view on the importance of occupational prestige for the definition of just wages, or they are guided by other considerations that are stronger than considerations related to the occupational prestige when ascribing just wages to the representatives of different professions.

Table 8.2 Actual and just monthly wages by occupation

Ukraine, UAH			Germany, EUR		
	Actual	Just		Actual	Just
Average monthly wage in 2009	1906	3949	Average monthly wage in 2008	3141	3302
Waiter	1267	3450	Manufacturing laborer	1 820	2288
Salesman	1565	3615	Doorman	2 303	2288
Hairdresser	1783	3453	Locomotive engine driver	2 595	3354
Builder	1511	4375	Administrative associate professional	2 631	2879
Bookkeeper	2231	3791	Hairdresser	1 305	2367
Doctor	1307	4394	Social work professional	2 426	2918
Journalist	1783	3945	Computer programmer	4 297	3544
University professor	1611	4180	Electrical engineer	5 109	3797
Entrepreneur	-	4121	General manager	5 094	4408
Lawyer	2231	4419	Medical doctor	6 031	5108

Source: Pracja Ukrajiny u 2009 roci (2010), Statistisches Bundesamt (2009), Omnibus 2009, SOEP Pretest 2008. The German data on actual monthly wages were available for 2006, while the SOEP Pretest survey was conducted in 2008. Since no data on the wages of single professions were available for Ukraine, the figures in the column "actual" wages represent the average monthly wages in the respective economic branches.

The apparent enormous differences between the just and actual wages in Ukraine reflect the high degree of injustice in the earnings distribution. While the just average monthly wages in Germany is only 5% higher than actual wages, in Ukraine, actual monthly wages constitute only 48% of the amount considered just by the population (figure 8.2).

Figure 8.2 Amount of injustice

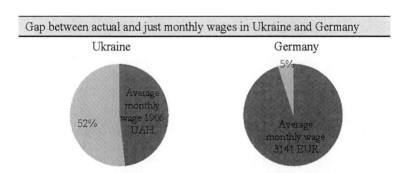

Gap between actual and just monthly wages in Ukraine and Germany

In a further step of analysis, I look at the ordering of the real criteria of the labor remuneration in Ukraine and Germany. The computation of the effects was undertaken by using the SOEP 2008 and Ukrainian Longitudinal Monitoring Survey 2004 datasets in the study of K. Auspurg, K. Gatskova and T. Hinz (2013). Figure 8.3 presents the semi-partial R-square values associated with the same characteristics that were used in the vignettes but applied to the actual earnings definition. General population surveys unfortunately provide no information on the work performance of the respondents and the effect of this important desert-related characteristic may not be assessed.

The first position in the hierarchy of the defining criteria of the labor remuneration in Germany is occupational prestige (Auspurg, Gatskova, Hinz 2013). In general, the conformity of the actual determinants of wages with the characteristics that should (according to people's justice judgments) determine the wages is relatively high if the importance of respondent's age and sex is ignored. The gender wage gap and higher incomes for older people are typical for Germany (Machin, Puhani 2003, Hinz, Gartner 2005, Welsh, Kühling 2013). Therefore, it is not surprising that these inequalities are reflected in the justice judgments of people, who (according to the adaptation theory) adjust their expectations to the social environment in a stable social system.

Figure 8.3 Actual distributive practices in Ukraine and Germany

Western Germany

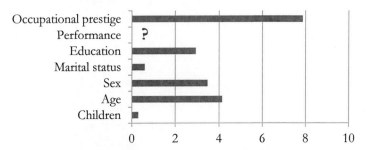

Eastern Germany

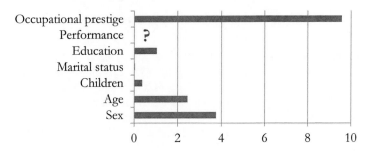

Ukraine

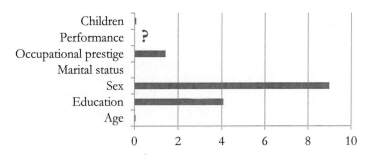

Source: Auspurg, Gatskova, Hinz (2013: 85).

The transformation process of Ukraine may not be characterized as a finished one; therefore, the adaptation of people's attitudes to a social environment has not yet taken place. The order of principles applied in justice judgments and order of the criteria applied for the attribution of earnings accordingly do not correspond to each other.

8.4 Factorial survey versus classic item-based measurement

In the same year of the factorial survey data collection in Ukraine, there was a first implementation of the ISSP survey on social inequality in this country. ISSP is a large-scale cross-country survey, which in 2009 concentrated on questions related to social stratification and inequality, social mobility, and distributive justice attitudes of people. Germany was among 40 countries that participated in this comparative survey project. The availability of the ISSP data for both Ukraine and Germany makes it possible to compare the obtained results coming from the factorial survey with those that rely on the classic item-based methods of attitudes measurement. This comparison allows not only to refine the findings on distributive justice attitudes, but also to highlight in which cases the implementation of the factorial survey design may be especially advantageous and relevant.

The questionnaire of the ISSP 2009 contains many interesting questions on distributive justice and inequality perception. Two blocks of questions are especially useful for the present study. The first block relates to the justice criteria that define just earnings of employees. The second block asks for assessments of the actual and just wages for several occupations in absolute terms. Table 8.3 presents the general overview of answers to these blocks of questions.

If to range the criteria of just pay according to the proportion of population who selected a corresponding criterion as an essential one, the crucial importance in both countries was ascribed to work performance (how well the job is done), hardworking, and responsibility associated with the job. All these characteristics are related to the desert justice principle. At the same time, the need related characteristics (family size, number of children) seem to be less important for the definition of fair wages in both countries.

Table 8.3 Assessing distributive justice in ISSP 2009

In deciding how much people ought to earn, how important should each of these things be, in your opinion; (in %)						
		Essen-tial	Very important	Fairly impor-tant	Not very impor-tant	Not important at all
How much responsibility goes with the job – how important do you think that ought to be in deciding pay?	UA	37.8	39.6	21.7	0.7	0.2
	DE	24.9	60.6	13.2	1.2	0.1
The number of years spent in education and training?	UA	27.7	33.5	33	4.4	1.4
	DE	9.8	46.8	34.1	8.2	1.1
What is needed to support a family?	UA	25.7	28.1	35.3	8.1	2.9
	DE	14.9	47.2	28.3	7.8	1.8
Whether the person has children to support – how important should that be in deciding pay?	UA	24.1	25.5	33.3	11	6.1
	DE	14.5	51	24.5	7.5	2.5
How well he or she does the job – how important should that be in deciding pay?	UA	44.5	38.7	15.7	0.7	0.5
	DE	26	63.1	10.1	0.7	0.1
How hard he or she works at the job?	UA	39.9	36.7	21.8	1.3	0.3
	DE	17.5	58.8	20.4	2.8	0.4

We would like to know what you think people in these jobs actually earn / Next, what do you think people in these jobs ought to be paid. How much do you think they should earn each regardless of what they actually get; (median values)

	UA (UAH, net per month)		DE (Euro, gross per month)	
	Actual	Just	Actual	Just
Doctor in general practice	1423.05	3000	5000	6000
Chairman of a large national corporation	10000	10000	20000	10000
Shop assistant	1000	2000	1500	2000
Unskilled worker in a factory	1000	2000	1300	1600
Cabinet minister in the national government	20000	7000	12000	8000

Source: ISSP 2009, author's computations.

Could we conclude that Ukrainians place more weigh on employees' responsibility or hardworking than Germans because a higher percentage of respondents in Ukraine selected the first ("essential") answer category? Perhaps not. The observed answer patterns rather suggest that Ukrainian respondents preferred to choose extreme values on the scale more often than German respondents. It means that there is a general difficulty for a comparative analysis of answers to these questions: respondents in different societies may use the same scale differently. In our case, German respondents are less inclined to choose the extreme answer categories. If a direct comparison of concrete justice principles between countries is problematic, it is still possible to establish the hierarchies of justice criteria within each country and then contrast them across countries. There is, however, a tricky difficulty in this approach. It lies in the fact that people were ascribing the importance to each of the criteria separately and as a result all criteria were considered as important to some extent by more than 80% of the population. Under these conditions, it is not easy to determine the importance of each criterion compared to one another. Furthermore, it is not clear whether people assess the same justice principles differently, when confronted with real-life situations where different considerations may show up in combinations.

At first sight it may seem that the results of the ISSP 2009 contradict those of the factorial survey in Ukraine. The respondents were strongly need-oriented when assessing the vignettes, and are overwhelmingly desert-oriented while judging the importance of justice principles in abstract terms. In fact, the differences are likely to be caused by the situations people deal with: in the case of ascribing the importance to the items, people evaluate abstract principles and when they assess the justice of incomes taken from real income distribution, they express justice judgments about specific state of affairs. There is no indication of an amount of earnings in the questions of ISSP 2009 and, hence, people may think of different sums when reflecting on importance of distributive justice criteria. If respondents consider the wages that are higher than the social minimum, their answers do not contradict the findings of the factorial survey. The disadvantage of the classic item-based approach to attitudes measurement in this case is that this approach leaves too much space for interpretation of answers and the knowledge gained from these answers is too general and abstract. Factorial survey approach on the contrary allows estimating the relative weight of each factor based on assessments of concrete situations.

The second block of questions presented in table 8.3 [3] measures people's estimations of actual and just wages in different occupations. There is only one profession in the list, which was used both in ISSP 2009 and the factorial survey module of the Omnibus 2009 – a medical doctor. The direct comparison of the mean just earnings for this occupation reveals a remarkable correspondence: in ISSP 2009 the just wages of a doctor was estimated as 4277.34 UAH, while the one assessed on the basis of the factorial survey was 4394 UAH. This finding additionally points to the reliability of the estimation results.

In both countries there is a common tendency towards equalizing of wages: people believe that those at the bottom of the income hierarchy should earn more, and those at the top, correspondingly, less. Accordingly, the assessment of just wages of medical doctors, shop assistants and unskilled workers is higher than the assessment of their actual earnings. On the other hand, the just wages of political and business elites should, according to respondents' evaluations, be lower than the earnings people believe the representatives of these occupations get. Interestingly, in both countries chairmen of large national companies are allowed to have higher earnings than cabinet ministers in the national government, although in

---

[3] Because the outliers – especially in German sample – cause considerable distortions of the means the table presents the median values and not the mean values. The mean values for Ukrainian sample may be found in table 3.1.

Ukraine, people believe that in reality the latter receive higher wages than the former. It means that people ascribe higher just wages to those, who are involved in the production of wealth, and not those, who administrate it.

Another interesting answer pattern is observed especially distinctly in the German case. Despite lowering the highest incomes and increasing the lowest ones while ascribing the just wages, respondents keep the hierarchy of occupations unchanged. In the end distribution of the just wages, all occupations are ranked in the same order as they are ranked in a distribution of actual wages: an unskilled worker, according to respondents' assessments, should earn less than a shop assistant, whose just wages is lower than that of a medical doctor etc. This finding supports the adaptation thesis, which stresses the shaping effect of existing inequalities for people's justice perception.

A general look at the disparities between actual and just wages reveals that in jobs where the just wages are higher than the actual ones (unskilled worker, shop assistant and doctor in general practice), the gap is much wider in Ukraine than in Germany. While in Germany the just wages in perception of respondents should be about one fifth higher than the actual earnings, the gap in Ukraine amounts up to 50%. This result suggests that in Ukraine the injustice in earnings is felt more acutely, what perfectly corresponds to the results of factorial survey analysis.

8.5 Critical remarks

It should be noted that like all other empirical research, the analysis presented in this monograph has restrictions. First of all, it should be taken into account that the explanation model of justice attitudes may not be limited only to the factors treated in this study. Because the research design of the Ukrainian study was developed, among others, following the idea of a comparative analysis with the German SOEP-Pretest survey, the vignette module was accordingly adjusted in order to enhance the comparability of results. At the same time, some dimensions that might have been important for the analysis of the justice evaluations were omitted. One should not, however, forget that the character of the social structure typical for post-Soviet transforming states differs considerably from the welfare systems found in Western democracies, and this implies many nuances in the distribution and redistribution systems and, consequently, in the perception of related phenomena by the population. In the following, I consider several details that should be taken into account when interpreting the results of the present study.

The vignettes asked respondents about their evaluation of gross earnings. In Germany, this indication is very important since the level of income tax depends not only on the level of earnings but also on family composition. In 2009, Ukraine had an inflexible tax rate of 15% for all working citizens. That is, the indication of "gross earnings" in the questionnaire informed a respondent that the earnings considered were actually 15% lower. The majority of Ukrainians perceive taxes as some kind of a tribute or kickback to the state and not as a necessary element of the redistribution system. According to the results of the social survey conducted by the Razumkov Center in 2009, answering the question "What do you feel when you pay taxes?," 37.9% of respondents (N=2012) said that they believed this money would be stolen by bureaucrats, 28% answered that they felt their honestly earned money was taken away from them, while 17.6% believed this money would not be stolen but rather redistributed in the wrong way, and a relatively small percentage of the population (15.5%) perceived taxes as a necessary mechanism of the social security system (Doslidžennia 2009).

A further peculiarity that might make the comparison of results between countries more complicated is the concept of salary itself. In contrast to the notions of "net" or "gross" earnings widely applied in Germany, Ukrainians are accustomed to thinking about their income in terms of basic wage rate and a range of different kinds of bonuses, increments, extra payments and in-kind advantages. Therefore, there is some room for interpretations if the word "salary" appears in the vignettes without further explanation. Moreover, a substantial feature of the post-communist societies is the widespread practice of informal economic behavior, which is so deeply rooted in the mechanisms of personal interactions that it is rather difficult to account for the impact of related considerations on justice judgment.

CHAPTER NINE

CONCLUSIONS

Scholars have shown that individual justice beliefs are highly relevant to a wide range of social phenomena. Since attitudes towards justice have an impact on individual actions and subjective wellbeing, they define structural characteristics of society (e.g., inequalities that are tolerated), legitimacy of political systems and persistence of social order in the long run.

The research presented in this book contributes to the empirical justice research in post-Soviet countries. The main aim of this study was to explore the mechanisms of the formation of justice attitudes through analysis of subjective justice evaluations related to a range of actual earnings in Ukraine. In order to uncover a complex structure of the justice principles that shape people's views on what they consider to be just, the innovative factorial survey design was applied. Integrating the principles of experimental design with those of the social survey, factorial survey method enabled the collection of multiple justice evaluations of actual earnings in Ukraine from 1797 respondents. This provided a unique empirical basis to investigate the simultaneous impact of different personal, family and enterprise characteristics of a fictitious employee on the amount of his or her just earnings and, in this way, to assess the weight placed on the considerations of need, desert and equality in the process of judging just earnings.

The study was conducted within the methodological approach of analytical sociology and incorporated the theoretical elaborations of such normative justice theories as multiprinciple justice theory, equity theory, status value theory, G. Jasso's theory and others. The combination of the major statements of the human capital, labor market, rational choice, socialization, adaptation, and cognitive dissonance theories with the analysis of the current political and socio-economic situation in Ukraine enabled the formulation of multiple hypotheses that were tested using the contextual and comparative perspectives of research.

Empirical analysis revealed that there exist a number of accepted inequities in Ukrainian society. One of the most salient of them is a just gender wage gap approved by both male and female respondents. Ukrainians consider higher wages for male fictitious persons to be just even if all other characteristics are held constant (educational attainment, occupation, work performance, etc.). This finding supports the suggestion concerning widespread support of the traditionalistic model of gender roles, which prescribes the role of the family's primary breadwinner to the male. In other words, the results of an empirical analysis demonstrate that the actual gender gap in earnings and the traditionalistic socialization patterns shape the justice judgments of Ukrainians, making them perceive gender inequality as just. This implies that a traditional model of gender roles (e.g., a male breadwinner and female housekeeper) is dominant in the mass consciousness of Ukrainians, and it is reflected in their justice judgments.

Ukrainian women expected lower just wages for female fictitious persons as compared to the expectations of men. I explain this empirical result as a consequence of a simultaneous operation of two mechanisms. On the one hand, there is the traditional gender socialization mechanism that makes Ukrainian citizens become rather conservative bearers of traditional gender roles. On the other hand, this finding provides support to the reference group comparison thesis, which would predict that women's expectations towards their earnings correspond to the real earnings of their reference group, which, under the conditions of labor market segregation, consists predominantly of other women.

An assumption drawn from the human capital and labor market theories stating that investment in human capital should be positively associated with the level of labor remuneration was supported by the data. Although Ukrainians did not take educational attainment of the vignette persons into account when defining just incomes, they were strongly guided by information on the work performance of the fictitious employees. There was no consecutive order in evaluations of just earnings according to the occupation indicated in a vignette, which probably reveals, among others, the overlooked impact of informal economic practices deeply embedded in the daily life of Ukrainians. However, the effect of work performance, which is the second largest effect in the model after that related to number of children, stresses the importance of desert considerations to the understanding of justice among Ukrainian citizens. The analysis of the processes in the educational system under transformation suggests that the human capital theory provides a valid explanation of the respondents' justice judgments, but that formal educational attainment is not a relevant measure of human capital in modern Ukraine.

The need principle dominated the judgments of Ukrainians across all population groups: people ascribed in the first place higher earnings to those with a greater need. The information on the number of children and employed persons in a family were considered particularly heavily by respondents.

Empirical analysis revealed that even though Ukrainians demonstrate some degree of tolerance for variation in earnings by ascribing the evaluation of "just" to quite a large number of vignettes, the largest part of actual official incomes in Ukraine are generally considered to be extremely low and do not correspond to the expectations of Ukrainians towards just amounts of earnings. However, if one excludes the three smallest income values used in the vignettes, the distribution of the vignettes' evaluations would be more balanced. Empirical evidence hints strongly that the earnings scale related to the percentiles of actual earnings' distribution of fulltime employees in Ukraine is, from the perspective of justice, strongly skewed to the left. This means that the actual earnings that correspond to the values of the first quintile of the income continuum are associated with poverty, which is a considerable problem plaguing modern Ukrainian society.

The dominance of need criterion in judgments on income justice clarifies that the current political and socio-economic challenges of the modern Ukrainian state (including high poverty rates, deficiency of the social security system and huge income inequalities) affect the vision of justice of Ukrainian respondents. However, need criteria lose their relative significance at the expense of the desert principle as soon as rather large income amounts are considered. This finding, in turn, leads to the suggestion that need considerations in the post-Soviet countries appear to be popular inasmuch as they find support among the low-income population and not because of the effect of the Soviet ideology. The empirical results support the argument of Boulding (1962) concerning need and desert principles, according to which the merit considerations first come into play after income amounts larger than the social minimum, as defined by people's needs, are treated.

The assumption that justice judgments also depend on some kind of restrictions given by external conditions in the enterprise was also confirmed by the data. That is, if there exists an opportunity to receive higher incomes because the enterprise achieves high revenues, then larger wages are considered just. On the contrary, if an enterprise faces risk of bankruptcy, the vignette persons are slightly more likely to be regarded as overpaid. The actual higher salaries in private companies similarly make respondents expect larger earnings amounts for the fictitious persons employed in the private sector as compared to those working for state enterprises.

A comparative perspective revealed that German respondents primarily take information on the person's desert (job-related characteristics) into account when defining just earnings. Contrary to Ukraine, the need considerations in Germany, although significant, play a relatively small role in the process of judging distributive justice. I argued that the weak social security system in Ukraine might contribute to people's shifting the responsibility for their wellbeing from the state to the employer. In Germany, by contrast, a high living standard and a developed system of social security are likely to make people distinguish between the responsibilities of the employer and the state: the social welfare system cares for people's basic needs, and the employer rewards their merits.

The results of justice attitudes analyses assert that the distributive justice is a complex and multidimensional phenomenon, which cannot be reduced to a single dimension or rule. While expressing justice judgments people rely on diverse information about the concrete situation and consider various criteria of fair distribution. In many cases justice judgments are the result of a search for a balance between merit, need and equality considerations. Although the weight put on justice principles may differ across countries or social groups within a society, it is remarkable that the mechanisms of justice attitudes formation seem to be universal. The results of the factorial survey studies in Ukraine and Germany suggest that people strongly consider self-interest arguments and in general adapt to the social environment they live in. During the socialization period they learn to justify particular wealth inequalities and internalize social roles and norms that lead to the reproduction of traditional inequalities based on gender, ethnic and other types of discrimination.

If mechanisms of justice attitudes formation have the same nature, what accounts for the different outcomes in justice judgments of people? The study, presented in this book provides empirical evidence that crucial importance in explaining the differences between justice judgments of people belongs to the different institutional contexts established in the course of the development of society. People naturally judge on what they believe the justice is based on what they observe around them. Social environments have a crucial effect on justice judgments of people because the actual state of affairs serves as a point of reference when defining just earnings. Accordingly, people in stable social systems are likely to adjust their justice attitudes to reality, while justice judgments of people from transforming societies are marked by a higher degree of uncertainty.

Many previous findings of empirical justice research are in line with the results of the present study. One of these findings relates to the fundamental aspiration of people to secure a social minimum, which guarantees the satisfaction of basic needs to every person irrespective of his merits and needs. As a result, in the countries with a high standard of living where social minimum is secured for all by the state, the crucial importance for justice evaluation of earnings is associated with the desert criterion. At the same, time in poorer countries, people are mostly concerned with survival practices and activities aimed at reaching a sustainable income security. Not surprisingly, in such a setting, considerations of need gain much higher importance. Under the conditions of widespread poverty, the idea of a social minimum gives the population major expectations towards just distribution of earnings.

Empirical findings of the study presented in this book advance not only scientific research on distributive justice but have also important implications for political and public debates in post-Soviet countries.

The acceptance and justification of economic inequalities in population have a crucial importance for the legitimacy of political order as well as for the reproduction of existing social structures. The huge discrepancy between real and perceived as fair wages in Ukraine signals that there is a high level of dissatisfaction about wealth distribution. This high level of perceived injustice may be considered as threatening the political stability in the country, where the state is apparently not able to provide an adequate standard of living for its citizens. In other words, the level of injustice perception may serve as an indicator of the degree of conflict potential in a society. From this perspective, the conspicuous level of perceived injustice uncovered in Ukraine indicates a high risk that under certain conditions the population will actively protest against the existing order.

Justice judgments of people in Ukraine send a distinct signal to the policy makers that there is a strong demand for redistribution and an urgent need for reforms of the labor market institutions and the welfare system. The high degree of consensus on the primary importance of the need justice principle reveals people's preferences for a more sophisticated and effective social policy. First of all, attention should be paid to the support of large families with three and more children. This is an important issue, which will have positive effects on achievements in other policy dimensions. For instance, demographic policy directed towards prevention of the population decline will be more effective if having children is not associated with poverty. The fact that the overwhelming majority of citizens clearly manifest their strong support for the guaranteed social minimum points to a large demand for improvement of the poverty alleviation policy. Obviously, the distributive mechanisms reforms should include in the first place a reform of the tax system. This means not only modernization of the taxation of individual incomes (e.g., progressive tax instead of flat rate tax), but also creation of better conditions for the development of small and middle enterprises. Currently, justice judgments of people demonstrate that people see employers in patriarchal terms: they are expected to care for people's needs. It means that the old Soviet perception of the relationship between employer (state) and individual has not yet been replaced. By stimulating the development of the small and middle enterprises it is possible to motivate people to take a more active role in managing their life. Apart from having positive effects on the economic development and life quality, such change in attitude towards personal responsibility for the course of one's own life is a necessary precondition for the development of civic culture and democratization.

Another policy-relevant aspect of the study is the common support of the merit justice principle. Although multiple studies stress that Ukraine nowadays is far from being a meritocracy, people in general believe that individual performance should be rewarded.

It is well known that the most fruitful ground for abundant discrimination appears in cases where the merit principle is ignored. If job positions in a professional hierarchy are allocated not according to the level of competence, but rather based on informal social networks, discrimination practices are likely to flourish. In the long run, discrimination on the labor market leads to such negative consequences as low efficiency of the economy and restricted prospects of economic development. Implementation of the meritocratic procedures of job allocation, such as open competitions with transparent selection procedures, will not only supply employers with a better-qualified staff but also raise the demand in the population for the better education and in this way stimulate reforms in the educational system.

It is remarkable, that people in Ukraine do not associate real human capital with the formal educational degree. This finding points to a serious problem in the educational system: according to people's views, formal educational degree is not always associated with the real productivity and professionalism, which means that educational institutions do not provide relevant knowledge, skills and competences that are required in the labor market. This finding suggests that government efforts should be placed, among other things, on solving the problem of skills mismatch.

The study of distributive justice attitudes helps to better understand people's perceptions that underlie the resistance to or support of changes implied by potential reforms. From this perspective, comprehensive knowledge of people's distributive justice attitudes creates a basis for the anticipation of possible difficulties or, on the contrary, favorable conditions for the implementation of relevant governmental programs.

The disclosure of mechanisms of justice attitudes formation in Ukraine is a first step towards explanation of manifold transition-related macro phenomena found in post-Soviet countries. It was beyond the scope of this book to ultimately explain any specific social phenomenon caused by actions (and interaction mechanisms) that were inspired by such attitudes. This kind of questions is left open for further research.

REFERENCES

Aalberg, T. (2003). Achieving Justice: Comparative Public Opinion on Income Distribution. Boston: Brill.

Abraham, M., T. Hinz, (eds.) (2005). Arbeitsmarktsoziologie. Probleme, Theorien, empirische Befunde. Wiesbaden: VS Verlag für Sozialwissenschaften.

Acock, A.C. (2008). A Gentle Introduction to Stata. Texas: Stata Press.

Alexander, C. S., H. J. Becker (1978). The Use of Vignettes in Survey Research. Public Opinion Quarterly, Vol. 42, No. 1, 93-104.

Ališev, B., O. Anikeenok (2007). Studenty o spravedlivosti v sfere raspredelenija. (Studens about distributive justice). Sociologičeskie issledovanija, No. 11, 103-110.

Almond, G. A., S. Verba (1963). The Civic Culture. Princeton: Princeton University Press.

Alpizar, F., F. Carlsson, O. Johansson-Stenman (2005). How much do we care about absolute versus relative income and consumption? Journal of Economic Behaviour and Organization. Vol. 56, 405-421.

Alves, W.M., P.H. Rossi (1978). The American Journal of Sociology, Vol. 84, No. 3, 541-564.

Alwin, D. F., G. Gornev, L. Khakhulina (1995). Comparative Referential Structures, System Legitimacy, and Justice Sentiments: An International Comparison. In: J. R. Kluegel, D. S. Mason, B. Wegener (eds.). Social Justice and Political Change: Public Opinion in Capitalist and Post-Communist States. NY: Walter de Gruyter, 109-130.

Appelbaum, M., M. C. Lenon, J. L. Aber (2006). When Effort is Threatening: The Influence of the Belief in a Just World on Americans' Attitudes Toward Antipoverty Policy. Political Psychology, Vol. 27, No. 3, 387-402.

Arabsheibani, G.R., A. Mussurov (2007). Returns to schooling in Kazakhstan. OLS and instrumental variables approach. Economics of Transition, Vol. 15, No. 2, 341-364.

Aristei, D., C. Perugini (2010). Preferences for redistribution and inequality in well-being across Europe. Journal of Policy Modeling, Vol. 32, No. 2, 176-195.

Arts, W. (1985). To each his due: ideas of social justice and Dutch income (re)distribution policy. The Netherland's Journal of Sociology, Vol. 21-2, 140-149.

Arts, W., P. Hermkens, P. van Wijck, (1991). Income and the idea of justice: principles, judgments, and their framing. Journal of Economic Psychology Vol. 12, No. 1, 121-140.

Arthur, J., W. H. Shaw (1978). Justice and Economic Distribution. Englewood Cliffs, N.J.: Prentice-Hall.

Atkinson, A. B., J. Micklewright (1992). Economic transformation in Eastern Europe and the distribution of income. Cambridge: Cambridge University Press.

Attwood, L. (1990). The New Soviet Man and Woman. Sex-Role Socialization in the USSR. Basingstoke: Macmillan.

Auspurg, K. (2010). Die Analyse sozialer Ungleichheit. Konzeptuelle Überlegungen und empirische Erkenntnisse. Dissertation. Universität Konstanz.

Auspurg, K., K. Gatskova, T. Hinz (2013). Vorstellungen von Lohngerechtigkeit in West- und Ostdeutschland und in der Ukraine. WSI Mitteilungen 2/2013, 77-88.

Auspurg, K., M. Abraham, T. Hinz (2009). Die Methodik des Faktoriellen Surveys in einer Paarbefragung. In: P. Kriwy, Ch. Gross (Hrsg.). Klein aber fein! Quantitative empirische Sozialforschung mit kleinen Fallzahlen. Wiesbaden: VS, Verlag für Sozialwissenschaften.

Auspurg, K., T. Hinz, S. Liebig (2009). Komplexität von Vignetten, Lerneffekte und Plausibilität im Faktoriellen Survey. Methoden – Daten – Analysen, Jg. 3, Heft 1, 59-96.

Auspurg, K., T. Hinz, S. Liebig, C. Sauer (2008). Wer verdient welches Einkommen? Ergebnisse eines Faktoriellen Surveys zur Einkommensgerechtigkeit in Deutschland. Universität Bielefeld/ Universität Konstanz.

Auspurg, K., A. Jäckle (2012). First equals most important? Order effects in vignette-based measurement. ISER working paper No. 2012-01.

Babenko, S. (2009). Social'na nerivnist' v ocinkah naselennja Ukrajiny za rezultatamy mižnarodnoho doslidžennja ISSP 2009 roku. (Assessments of social inequality in Ukraine based on ISSP 2009) Kyiv: IS NASU.

Balakirjeva O. M., Černenko S.M. (2009). Nerivnomirnist' dohodiv naselennja Ukrajiny jak social'no-ekonomična problema. (Income inequality in Ukraine as a socio-economic problem) Ukrajins'kyj socium, Vol. 3, No. 30, 49-64.

Barrington, L. W. (2002). Examining rival theories of demographic influences on political support: The power of regional, ethnic, and linguistic divisions in Ukraine. European Journal of Political Research, Vol. 41, No. 4, 455-491.

Barrington, L. W., Faranda R. (2009). Reexamining Region, Ethnicity, and Language in Ukraine. Post-Soviet Affairs, Vol. 25, No. 3, 232-256.

Barsukova, S. (2003). Formal'no i neformal'no trudoustroennye rabotniki – ravenstvo ili neravenstvo položenija? (Employed officially or informally – are there inequalities of positions?). In: Ryvkina, R. (ed.). Spravedlivye i nespravedlivye social'nie neravenstva v sovremennoy Rossii (Just and unjust social inequalities in modern Russia). Moscow: Referendum, 384-409.

Baum, H. (2004). Theorien sozialer Gerechtigkeit. Politische Philosophie für soziale Berufe. Münster: Lit Verlag.

Beck, M., K.-D. Opp (2001). Der Faktorielle Survey und die Messung von Normen. Kölner Zeitschrift für Soziologie und Sozialpsychologie, Vol. 53, No. 2, 283-306.

Becker, G. S. (1964). Human Capital. A Theoretical and Empirical Analysis, with Special Reference to Education. New York: Columbia University Press.

Bentham, J. (1965). Introduction to the Principles of Morals and Legislation. New York: Hafner Publishing Co.

Bentler, P. M., C.-P. Chou (1987). Practical Issues in Structural Modeling. Sociological Methods and Research, Vol. 16, No. 1, 78-117.

Berger, J., M. Zelditch, B. Anderson, B. P. Cohen (1972). Structural aspects of distributive justice: a status value formulation. In: Berger et al. (eds.). Sociological Theories in Progress, Volume 2. Boston: Houghton Mifflin.

Bezrukova, K., Ch. S. Spell, J. L. Perry (2010). Violent Splits or Healthy Divides? Coping with Injustice through Faultlines. Personnel Psychology, Vol. 63, 719-751.

Bohner, G., M. Wänke (2009). Attitudes and Attitude Change. East Sussex: Psychology Press.

Boudon, R. (1998). Social Mechanisms without Black Boxes. In: P. Hedström, R. Swedberg (eds.). Social Mechanisms. An Analytical Approach to Social Theory. NY: Cambridge University Press.

Boulding, K. E. (1962). Social Justice in Social Dynamics. In: Brandt, R. B. (ed.). Social Justice. Englewood Cliffs: Prentice-Hall, 73-92.

Brainerd, E. (1998). Winners and Losers in Russia's Economic Transition. The American Economic Review, Vol. 88, No. 5, 1094-1116.

Brainerd, E. (2000). Women in Transition: Changes in Gender Wage Differentials in Eastern Europe and the Former Soviet Union. Industrial and Labor Relations Review, Vol. 54, No. 1, 138-162.

Brickman, P., R. Folger, E. Goode, Y. Schul (1981). Microjustice and Macrojustice. In: Lerner, M. J., S. C. Lerner (eds.), The Justice Motive In Social Behavior. Adapting to Times of Scarcity and Change, 173-202.

Brück, T., A. M. Danzer, A. Muravyev, N. Weisshaar, (2010). Poverty during transition: Household survey evidence from Ukraine. Journal of Comparative Economics, 38 (2), 123-145.

deCarufel, A. (1981). The Allocation and Acquisition of Resources in Times of Scarcity. In: Lerner, M. J., S. C. Lerner (eds.), The Justice Motive In Social Behavior. Adapting to Times of Scarcity and Change, 317-341.

Cheren'ko, L. (2008). The Regional Dimensions of Poverty in Ukraine. Problems of Economic Transition, Vol. 51, No. 7, 29-35.

Choi, S. (2011). Organizational Justice and Employee Work Attitudes: The Federal Case. The American Review of Public Administration, Vol. 41, No. 2, 185-204.

Clark, A. E., P. Frijters, M. A. Shields (2008). Relative Income, Happiness, and Utility: An Explanation for the Easterlin Paradox and Other Puzzles. Journal of Economic Literature. Vol. 46, No. 1, 95-144.

Clay-Warner, J., K. A. Hegtvedt, P. Roman (2005). Procedural Justice, Distributive Justice: How Experiences with Downsizing Condition Their Impact on Organizational Commitment. Social Psychology Quarterly, Vol. 68, No. 1, 89-102.

Clem, R. S., P. R. Craumer (2008). Orange, Blue and White, and Blonde: The Electoral Geography of Ukraine's 2006 and 2007 Rada Elections. Eurasian Geography and Economics, Vol. 49, No. 2, 127-151.

Cohen-Charash, Yo., P. E. Spector (2001). The Role of Justice in Organizations: a Meta-Analysis. Organizational Behavior and Human Decision Processes, Vol. 86, No. 2, 278–321.

Cohn, E. S., S. O. White, J. Sanders (2000). Distributive and procedural justice in seven nations. Law and Human Behavior, Vol. 24, No. 5, 553-578.

Coleman, J. (1994). Foundations of Social Theory. Cambrigde: Harvard University Press.

Coleman, J. (1986). Social Theory, Social Research, and a Theory of Action. American Journal of Sociology, Vol. 91, No. 6, 1309-1335.

Diekmann, A., Eichner K., Schmidt P., Voss T. (Hrsg.) (2008). Rational Choice: Theoretische Analysen und empirische Resultate. Wiesbaden: VS, Verlag für Sozialwissenschaften.

Delhey, J. (2001). Osteuropa zwischen Marx und Markt. Soziale Ungleichheit und soziales Bewußtsein nach dem Kommunismus. Hamburg: Krämer.

Demchuk, P., V. Zelenyuk (2009). Testing differences in efficiency of regions within a country: the case of Ukraine. Journal of Productivity Analysis. Vol. 32, No. 2, 81-102.

Deržavnyj komitet statystyky Ukrajiny (State Statistics Service of Ukraine), (http://www.ukrstat.gov.ua/), retrieved on 16.06.2013.

Deutsch, M. (1975). Equity, equality, and need: What determines, which value will be used as the basis of distributive justice? Journal of Social Issues, Vol. 31, No. 3, 137-149.

Dopovid' "Henderni aspekty rynku praci v Ukrajini" (Gender aspects of labor market in Ukraine) (2011). State Statistics Service of Ukraine.

Doslidžennia: Deržava spryjaje social'nij nerivnosti v Ukrajini (2009). (The State favors social inequality in Ukraine). Dzerkalo tyžnja #9 (737), 14-20 bereznja 2009.

Douglas, M. (1978). Cultural bias. Occasional paper No. 35. London: Royal Anthropological Institute of Great Britain and Ireland.

Düppen, B. (1996). Der Utilitarismus: eine theoriegeschichtliche Darstellung von der griechischen Antike bis zur Gegenwart. Inauguraldissertation, Universität Köln.

Easterlin, R. A. (1995). Will raising the incomes of all increase the happiness of all? Journal of Economic Behavior and Organization, Vol. 27, No. 1, 35-47.

Elster, J. (2010). Explaining Social Behavior. More Nuts and Bolts for the Social Sciences. Cambridge: Cambridge University Press.

—. (1995). The empirical study of justice. In Miller, D., and Walzer, M. (eds.). Pluralism, Justice and Equality. New York: Oxford University Press, 81-98.

ESS 2004-2012. European Social Survey. Database, available at: http://www.europeansocialsurvey.org/data/country.html?c=ukraine, retrieved on 31.08.2014.

Esser, H. (1993). Soziologie. Spezielle Grundlagen. Band 1: Situationslogik und Handeln. Frankfurt-am-Main: Campus.

—. (1999). Soziologie. Allgemeine Grundlagen. Frankfurt-am-Main: Campus.

—. (2000). Soziologie. Spezielle Grundlagen. Band 5: Institutionen. Frankfurt-am-Main: Campus.

—. (2001). Soziologie. Spezielle Grundlagen. Band 6: Sinn und Kultur. Frankfurt-am-Main: Campus.

Evans, M. D. R., J. Kelley (2004). Subjective Social Location: Data from 21 Nations. International Journal of Public Opinion Research, Vol. 16, No. 1, 3-38.

Festinger, L. (1957). A Theory of Cognitive Dissonance. Stanford: Stanford University Press.

Forsé, M., M. Parodi (2007). Perception des Inégalités Économique et sentiment de Justice Sociale. Revue de l'OFCE, Vol. 102, 483-540.

Fleisher, B. M., K. Sabirianova, X. Wang (2005). Returns to Skills and the Speed of Reforms: Evidence from Central and Eastern Europe, China, and Russia. Journal of Comparative Economics, Vol. 33, No. 2, 351-370.

Frohlich, N., J. A. Oppenheimer (1992). Choosing Justice. An Experimental Approach to Ethical Theory. Berkeley: University of California Press.

Ganguli, I., K. Terell (2005). Wage Ceilings and Floors: The Gender Gap in Ukraine's Transition. IZA Discussion Paper No. 1776, September 2005.

Gatskova, K. (2013). Distributive Justice Attitudes in Ukraine: Need, Desert or Social Minimum? Communist and Post-Communist Studies, Vol. 46, No. 2, 227-241.

Gatskova, K., M. Gatskov (2012). The Weakness of Civil Society in Ukraine: A Mechanism-Based Explanation. IOS Working Paper No. 323.

Gavrilova, I. (2009). Zapadnye traktovki socialnoj spravedlivosti. Obzor koncepcyj. (Western interpretations of social justice. An overview). Sociologičesie issledovanija, No. 3, 36-44.

Gebel, I. Kogan (2011). When Higher Education Pays Off: Education and Labor Market Entry in Ukraine. In: Kogan, I., C. Noelke, M. Gebel (eds.). Making the Transition: Education and Labor Market Entry in Central and Eastern Europe. Stanford: Stanford Univ. Press.

Gijsberts, M. (2002). The Legitimation of Income Inequality in State-Socialist and Market Societies. Acta Sociologica, Vol. 45, No. 4, 269-285.

Granovetter, M., R. Soong (1983). Threshold Models of Diffusion and Collective Behavior. Journal of Mathematical Sociology, Vol. 9, No. 3, 165-79.

Greenberg, J. (1990). Employee Theft as a Reaction to Underpayment Inequality: The Hidden Costs of Pay Cuts. Journal of Applied Psychology, Vol. 75, No. 5, 561-568.

Gregory, P.R., J. E. Kohlhase (1988). The Earnings of Soviet Workers: Evidence from the Soviet Interview Project. The Review of Economics and Statistics, Vol. 70, No. 1, 23-35.

Golov, A., Ju. Levada (1993). Sovetskij prostoj čelovek. Opyt socialnogo portreta na rubeže 90-h. Moskva: Mirovoj Okean.

Golovakha, E., N. Panina (2009). Main Stages and Tendencies in Transformation of Ukrainian Society: from Perestroika to Orange Revolution. Ukrainian Sociological Review 2006–2007, 3-24.

Gorodnichenko, Yu., K. Sabirianova Peter (2007). Public Sector Pay and Corruption: Measuring Bribery from Micro Data. Journal of Public Economics, Vol. 91, No. 5-6, 963-991.

Grün, C., S. Klasen (2001). Growth, Income Distribution, and Well-Being in Transition Countries. Economics of Transition, Vol. 9, No. 2, 359-394.

Gudkov, L., B. Dubin, N. Zorkaya (2008). Postsovetskij čelovek i graždanskoe obščestvo. (Post-Soviet person and civil society). Moscow: Moskovskaja škola političeskih issledovanij.

Hadler, M. (2005). Why Do People Accept Different Income Ratios? A Multi-Level Comparison of Thirty Countries. Acta Sociologica, Vol. 48, No. 2, 131-154.

Hare, R. M. (1978). Justice and Equality. In: Arthur, J., Shaw, W.H. (eds.), Justice and Economic Distribution. Englewood Cliffs, New Jersey: Prentice-Hall, 116-131.

Harsanyi, J. C. (1976). Essays on Ethics, Social Behavior, and Scientific Explanation. Dordrecht, Holland: D. Reidel Publishing Company.

Hedström, P. (1994). Contagious Collectivities: On the Spatial Diffusion of Swedish Trade Unions, 1890-1940. American Journal of Sociology, Vol. 99, No. 5/1994: 1157-1179.

—. (2005). Dissecting the Social. On the Principles of Analytical Sociology. New York: Cambridge University Press.

Hedström, P., Y. Åberg (2005). Quantitative research, agent based modeling and theories of the social. In: Hedström, P. Dissecting the Social. On the Principles of Analytical Sociology. New York: Cambridge University Press.

Hedström, P., P. Bearman (eds.) (2011). The Oxford Handbook of Analytical Sociology. Oxford: Oxford University Press.

Hedström, P., R. Swedberg (eds.) (1998). Social Mechanisms. An Analytical Approach to Social Theory. NY: Cambridge University Press.

Hedström, P., P. Ylikoski (2014). Analytical sociology and rational choice theory. In: G. Manzo (ed.). Analytical sociology: actions and networks. Chichester: Wiley.

Hermkens, P. L. J. (1986). Fairness judgements of the distribution of incomes. The Netherland's Journal of Sociology, Vol. 22, 61-71.

Hermkens P. L. J., F. A. Boerman (1989). Consensus with respect to the Fairness of Incomes: Differences between Social Groups. Social Justice Research, Vol. 3, No. 3, 201-215.

Heyns, B. (2005). Emerging Inequalities in Central and Eastern Europe. Annual Review of Sociology, Vol. 31, 163-197.

Hinz, T., H. Gartner (2005). Geschlechtsspezifische Lohnunterschiede in Branchen, Berufen und Betrieben. The Gender Wage Gap within Economic Sectors, Occupations, and Firms. Zeitschrift für Soziologie, Jg. 34, Heft 1, 22–39.

Hodge, R. W., P. M. Siegel, P. H. Rossi (1964). Occupational Prestige in the United States, 1925-63. American Journal of Sociology. Vol. 70, No. 3, 286-302.

Homans, G. C. (1961). Social Behavior: Its Elementary Forms. New York: Harcourt, Brace, Jovanovich.

Homans, G. C. (1973). Social Behavior: Its Elementary Forms. London, Routledge & Kegan.

Hox J. J., I. G. G. Kreft, P. L. J. Hermkens. (1991). The Analysis of Factorial Surveys. Sociological Methods and Research, 19, 493-510.

Human Development Report Ukraine, 2008 (http://hdr.undp.org/en/ reports/national/europethecis/ukraine/name,3244,en.html), retrieved on 16.05.2013.

Institute of Sociology of the National Academy of Sciences of Ukraine (2009). Ukrajins'ke Suspil'stvo 1992-2009. Dynamika social'nyh zmin. [Ukrainian Society in 1992-2009. Dynamics of Social Changes] Kyiv: IS NANU, Azbuka.

ISSP 2009. International Social Survey programme, Social Inequality IV, database. http://zacat.gesis.org/webview/index.jsp?objectjhttp://zacat.gesis.org/o bj/fStudy/ZA5400. retrieved on 2.04.2013.

Ivaščenko, O. (2010). Ob anatomii ekonomičeskogo neravenstva v sovremennoj Ukraine: sociologičeskije opyty (On anatomy of economic inequality in modern Ukraine: sociological experiments). Sociologija: teorija, metody, marketing, 4, 29-55.erlag, 97-122.

Jacobs, J. (2006). Facetten sozialer Ungleichheit – Einstellungen zu Freihheit, Gleichheit und Gerechtigkeit im postkommunistischen

Europa. In: Osteuropas Bevölkerung auf dem Weg in die Demokratie, Wiesbaden: VS

Jann, B. (2003). Lohngerechtigkeit und Geschlechterdiskriminierung: Experimentelle Evidenz. ETH Zürich.

Jasso, G. (1978). On the Justice of Earnings: A New Specification of the Justice Evaluation Function. American Journal of Sociology. American Journal of Sociology, Vol. 83, 1398-1419.

—. (1980). A New Theory of Distributive Justice. American Sociological Review, Vol. 45, 3-32.

—. (1986). A New Representation of the Just Term in Distributive Justice Theory: Its Properties and Operation in Theoretical Derivation and Empirical Estimations. Journal of Mathematical Sociology, Vol. 12, Issue 3, 251-274.

—. (1994). Assessing Individual and Group Differences in the Sense of Justice: Framework and Application to Gender Differences in the Justice of Earnings. Social Science Research, 23, 368-406.

—. (2007). Studying justice: Measurement, Estimation, and Analysis of the Actual Reward and the Just Reward. IZA Discussion Paper No. 2592, January 2007, Bonn.

Jasso, G., K.-D. Opp (1997). Probing the character of norms: a factorial survey analysis of the norms of political action. American Sociological Review, Vol. 62, 947-964.

Jasso, G., P. H. Rossi (1977). Distributive Justice and Earned income. American Sociological Review, Vol. 42, 639-651.

Jasso, G., M. Webster Jr. (1997). Double Standards in Just Earnings for Male and Female Workers. Social Psychology Quarterly, Vol. 60, No. 1, 66-78.

Jasso, G., M. Webster Jr. (1999). Assessing the Gender Gap in Just Earnings and Its Underlying Mechanisms. Social Psychology Quarterly, Vol. 62, No. 4, 367-380.

Junisbai, A. K. (2010). Understanding economic justice attitudes in Two Countries: Kazakhstan and Kyrgyzstan. Social Forces, 88(4), 1677-1702.

Jurajda, S. (2003). Gender Wage Gap and Segregation in Enterprises and the Public Sector in Late Transition Countries. Journal of Comparative Economics, Vol. 31, No. 2, 199-222.

Kakwani, N. (1995). Income Inequality, Welfare and Poverty. An Illustration Using Ukrainian Data. Policy Research Working Paper 1411. The World Bank Policy Research Department.

—. (1996). Income Inequality, Welfare and Poverty in Ukraine. Development and Change. Vol. 27, No. 4, 663-691.

Karniol, R., D. T. Miller (1981). Morality and the Development of Conceptions of Justice. In: Lerner, M. J., S. C. Lerner (eds.), The Justice Motive In Social Behavior. Adapting to Times of Scarcity and Change, 73-89.

Katchanovski, I. (2006). Regional Political Divisions in Ukraine in 1991–2006. Nationalities Papers: The Journal of Nationalism and Ethnicity, Vol. 34, No. 5, 507-532.

Katz, K. (2001). Gender, Work and Wages in the Soviet Union. Basingstoke: Palgrave.

Kirjuchin, D., S. Ščerbak (2007). Predstavlenija o spravedlivosti v Rossii i v Ukraine: povsednevnost' i ideologija (Notions of justice in Russia and Ukraine: daily routine and ideology). Sociologija: teorija, metody, marketing, No. 1, 136-150.

Kivimäki, M., M. Elovainio, J. Vahtera, J. E. Ferrie (2003). Organisational Justice and Health of Employees: Prospective Cohort Study. Occupational and Environmental Medicine, Vol. 60, No. 1, 27-34.

Kluegel, J. R., D. S. Mason, (2004). Fairness Matters: Social Justice and Political Legitimacy in Post-Communist Europe, Europe-Asia Studies, Vol. 56, No. 6, 813–34.

Kluegel, J. R., D. S. Mason, B. Wegener (eds.) (1995). Social Justice and Political Change: Public Opinion in Capitalist and Post-Communist States. Berlin, New York: De Gruyter.

Knack, S., P. Keefer (1997). Does Social Capital Have an Economic Payoff? A Cross-Country Investigation. The Quarterly Journal of Economics, Vol. 112, No. 4, 1251-1288.

Komarova, O. (2008). Social'na spravedlyvist' jak osnovnyj pryncyp procesu rozpodilu social'nyh transfertiv. (Social justice as a main principle of distribution of social transfers). Ukrajins'kyj socium, No. 2, 106-112.

Kubicek, P. (2000). Regional Polarisation in Ukraine: Public Opinion, Voting and Legislative Behaviour. Europe-Asia Studies, Vol. 52, No. 2, 273-294.

Kuhfeld, W. F., R. D. Tobias, M. Garrat (1994). Efficient Experimental Design with Marketing Research Applications. Journal of Marketing Research, Vol. 31, No. 4, 545-557.

Legewie, J. (2008). Zum Einfluss regionaler Arbeitslosigkeit auf Einstellungen zur sozialen Gerechtigkeit. Kölner Zeitschrift für Soziologie und Sozialpsychologie, Vol. 60, No. 2, 286-313.

Lerner, M. J. (1981). The Justice Motive In Human Relations. Some Thoughts on What We Know and Need to Know about Justice. In:

Lerner, M. J., S. C. Lerner (eds.), The Justice Motive In Social Behavior. Adapting to Times of Scarcity and Change, 11-35.

Levada, Ju. (1993). Die Sowjetmenschen 1989 – 1991. Soziogramm eines Zerfalls. München: Dt. Taschenbuch-Verl.

Lewin-Epstein, N., A. Kaplan, A. Levanon (2003). Distributive Justice and Attitudes Toward the Welfare State. Social Justice Research, Vol. 16, No. 1, 1-27.

Liebig, S. (2001). Lessons from Philosophy? Interdisciplinary Justice Research and Two Classes of Justice Judgments. Social Justice Research, Vol. 14, No. 3, 265-287.

Liebig, S. (2002a). Gerechtigkeit in Organisationen: Theoretische Überlegungen und empirische Ergebnisse zu einer Theorie korporativer Gerechtigkeit. In: J. Allmendinger, T. Hinz (Hrsg.). Organisationssoziologie. Kölner Zeitschrift für Soziologie und Sozialpsychologie, Sonderheft 42, 151-187.

—. (2002b). Gerechtigkeitseinstellungen und Gerechtigkeitsurteile. Zur Unterscheidung zweier Urteilskategorien. In: S. Liebig, H. Lengfeld (Hrsg.). Interdisziplinäre Gerechtigkeitsforschung. Zur Verknüpfung Empirischer und Normativer Perspektiven. Frankfurt/New York: Campus Verlag.

—. (2007). Modelle und Befunde der Empirischen Gerechtigkeitsforschung in Deutschland am Beispiel der Einkommens- und Steuergerechtigkeit. In: Empter, S., R. B. Vehrkamp (Hrsg.). Soziale Gerechtigkeit – eine Bestandsaufnahme. Gütersloh: Verlag Bertelsmann Stiftung, 111-135.

Liebig, S., Mau S. (2005a). A Legitimate Guaranteed minimum Income? In: G. Standing (ed.) Promoting income security as a right: Europe and North America. London: Anthem Press.

Liebig, S., Mau S. (2005b). Wann ist ein Steuersystem gerecht? Einstellungen zu allgemeinen Prinzipien der Besteuerung und zur Gerechtigkeit der eigenen Steuerlast. Zeitschrift für Soziologie, Jg. 34, Heft 6, 468-491.

Liebig, S., C. Sauer, J. Schupp (2011). Die wahrgenommene Gerechtigkeit des eigenen Erwerbseinkommens: Geschlechtstypische Muster und die Bedeutung des Haushaltskontextes. Kölner Zeitschrift für Soziologie und Sozialpsychologie, Jg. 63(1), 33-59.

Likert, R. (1932). A Technique for the Measurement of Attitudes. Archives of Psychology, No. 140. New York: Columbia University.

Mahin, S., P. A. Puhani (2003). Subject of Degree and the Gender Wage Differential: Evidence from the UK and Germany. Economic Letters, Vol. 79, No. 3, 393-400.

Malyš, L. (2011). Obščeje i otličnoje v vosprijatii socialnogo neravenstva naselenijem raznyh stran. (Common and divergent features of inequality perception in different countries). Sociologija: teorija, metody, marketing, 4, 97-120.

Marshall, G., A. Swift, D. Routh, C. Burgoyne (1999). What is and what ought to be. Popular beliefs about distributive justice in thirteen countries. European Sociological Review, Vol. 15, No. 4, 349-367.

Mason, D. (1995). Justice, Socialism, and Participation in the Postcommunist States. In: Kluegel, J. R., D. Mason, B. Wegener (eds.). Social Justice and Political Change. Public Opinion in Capitalist and Post-Communist States. New York: De Gruyter, 49-80.

Mason, D. S., J. R. Kluegel (2000). Marketing Democracy: Changing Opinion about Inequality and Politics in East Central Europe. Lanham: Rowman & Littlefield Publishers.

Meltzer, A. H., S. F. Richard (1981). A Rational Theory of the Size of Government. Journal of Political Economy, Vol. 89, No. 5, 914-927.

Merton, R. K. (1967). On Theoretical Sociology. New York: The Free Press.

Michelbach, P. A., J. T. Scott, R. E. Matland, B. H. Borstein (2003). Doing Rawls Justice: An Experimental Study of Income Distribution Norms. American Journal of Political Science, Vol. 47, No. 3, 523-539.

Milanovic, B. (2000). The median-voter hypothesis, income inequality, and income redistribution: an empirical test with the required data. European Journal of Political Economy, Vol. 16, No. 3, 367-410

Miller, D. (1999). Principles of Social Justice. Cambridge, London: Harvard University Press.

Mincer, J. (1974). Schooling, Experience, and Earnings. New York: Columbia University Press.

Murphy, A., N. Levchuk, A. Stickley, B. Roberts, M. McKee (2013). A country divided? Regional variation in mortality in Ukraine. International Journal of Public Health (http://link.springer.com/article/10.1007/s00038-013-0457-2), retrieved on 16.05.2013.

Mykhnenko, V. (2010). Ukraine's Diverging Space-Economy: The Orange Revolution, Post-Soviet Development Models and Regional Trajectories. European Urban and Regional Studies, Vol. 17, No. 2, 141-165.

Nazarov, M. (1999). Social'naja spravedlivost': sovremennyj rossijskij kontekst. (Social justice: the context of modern Russia). Sociologičeskie issledovanija 11, 41-49.

Newell, A., B. Reilly (1996). The Gender Wage Gap in Russia. Some Empirical Evidence. Labour Economics, Vol. 3, 337-356.

Newell, A., B. Reilly (2001). The Gender Pay Gap in the Transition from Communism: Some empirical Evidence. Economic Systems, Vol. 25, 287-304.

Oishi, S., S. Kesebir, E. Diener (2011). Income Inequality and Happiness. Psychological Science, Vol. 22, No. 9, 1095-1100.

Oksamytna, S. (2010). Institucionalnaya sreda vosproizvodstva socialnogo neravenstva. (Institutional context of reproduction of social inequality). Sociologija: teorija, metody, marketing, No. 4, 4-28.

Oksamytna S., Khmelko V. (2007): Social Exclusion in Ukraine in an initial Stage of the Restoring Capitalism. Ukrainian Sociological Review, named after Natalia Panina, 2004-2005. Kyiv: IS NASU, 179-192.

Oksamytna S., Patrakova A. (2007). Ijerarchija prestyžnosti profesij i zanjat' (The hierarchy of professions' and occupations' prestige) / Ukrajins'ke suspil'stvo, Kyiv, IS NANU, 170-179.

Olson, M. (1968). Die Logik des Kollektiven Handelns. Kollektivgüter und die Theorie der Gruppen. Tübingen: J. C. B. Mohr.

Omnibus 2009. Database. Institute of Sociology of the National Academy of Sciences of Ukraine, Kyiv.

Osipian, A. L. (2009). Corruption and Reform in Higher Education in Ukraine. Canadian and International Education, Vol. 38, No. 2, 104-122.

Pailhé, A. (2000). Gender Discrimination in Central Europe during the Systemic Transition. Economics of Transition. Vol. 8, No. 2, 505-535.

Paniotto, V., N. Kharchenko (2008). What Poverty Criteria Are Best for Ukraine? Problems of Economic Transition, Vol. 51, No. 7, 5–12.

Perelli-Harris, B. (2008). Family Formation in Post-Soviet Ukraine: Changing Effects of Education in a Period of Rapid Social Change. Social Forces, Vol. 87, No. 2, 767-794.

Petersen, T. (1992). Individual, Collective, and Systems Rationality in Work Groups: Dilemmas and Market-Type Solutions. American Journal of Sociology, Vol. 98, No. 3, 469-510.

Pilyavsky, A., W. E. Aaronson, P. M. Bernet, M. D. Rosko, V. G. Valdmanis, M. V. Golubchikov (2006). East-west: does it make a difference to hospital efficiencies in Ukraine? Health Economics, Vol. 15, 1173-1186.

Pirogov, G., B. Efimov (2008). Social'naja spravedlivost': genesis idej. (Social justice: genesis of ideas). Sociologičeskie issledovanija 9, 3-11.

Polavieja, J. G. (2013). Socially Embedded Investments: Explaining Gender Differences in Job-Specific Skills. American Journal of Sociology, Vol. 118, No. 3, 592-634.

Polese, A. (2010). Doslidžennja riznoji pryrody nezakonnyh transakcij v Ukrajini (Study on the various nature of illegal transactions in Ukraine). Sociolohija: teorija, metody, marketynh 3, 52-70.

Pracja Ukrajiny u 2009 roci (2010). Statystyčnyj zbirnyk. (Employment in Ukraine in 2009. Statistics digest). State Statistics Service of Ukraine.

Randall, C. S., Mueller C. (1995). Extensions of Justice Theory: Justice Evaluations and Employees Reactions in a Natural Setting. Social Psychology Quarterly, Vol. 58, 178-194.

Raphael, D. D. (2001). Concepts of Justice. Oxford: Clarendon Press.

Rawls, J. (1972). A Theory of Justice. Oxford: Clarendon Press.

Rescher, N. (1966). Distributive Justice: A Constructive Critique of the Utilitarian Theory of Distribution. New York: The Bobbs-Merrill Company, Inc.

Rossi, P. H. (1951). The Application of Latent Structure Analysis to the Study of Social Stratification. Ph.D. dissertation, Columbia University.

Rossi, P. H. (1979). Vignette Analysis: Uncovering the Normative Structure of Complex Judgments. In: Merton, R. K., J. S. Coleman, P. H. Rossi (eds.), Qualitative and Quantitative Social Research: Papers in Honour of Paul F. Lazarsfeld. NY: The Free Press, 176-186.

Round, J., C. Williams (2010). Coping with the Social Costs of 'Transition': Everyday Life in Post-Soviet Russia and Ukraine. European Urban and Regional Studies, Vol. 17, No. 2, 183-196.

Round, J., C. C. Williams, P. Rodgers (2008). Corruption in the Post-Soviet Workplace: the Experiences of Recent Graduates in Contemporary Ukraine. Work, employment and Society. Vol. 22, No. 1, 149-166.

Rowland, R.H. (2004). National and Regional Population Trends in Ukraine: Results from the Most Recent Census. Eurasian Geography and Economics, Vol. 45, No. 7, 491-514.

Rydgren, J. (2011). Beliefs. In: The Oxford Handbook of Analytical Sociology / eds. P. Hedström, P. Bearman. Oxford: Oxford University Press.

Ryvkina, R. (ed.) (2003). Spravedlivye i nespravedlivye socialnie neravenstva v sovremennoy Rossii (Just and unjust social inequalities in modern Russia). Moscow: Referendum.

Saar, E. (2008). Different cohorts and evaluation of income differences in Estonia. International Sociology, Vol. 23, No. 3, 417-445.

Sabbagh, C. (2002). A Taxonomy of Normative and Empirically Oriented Theories of Distributive Justice. Social Justice Research, Vol. 14, No. 3, 237-263.

Sajenko, Ju. (ed.) (2007). Henderni stereotypy ta stavlennja hromads'kosti do hendernyh problem v Ukrajins'komu suspil'stvi. (Gender stereotypes and people's attitudes towards gender problems in Ukraine). Kyiv: Institute of Sociology of National Academy of Sciences.

Sauer, C. (2014). A Just Gender Pay Gap? Three Factorial Survey Studies on Justice Evaluation of Earnings for Male and Female Employees. SFB 882, Working Paper No. 29.

Sauer, C., K. Auspurg, T. Hinz, S. Liebig, J. Schupp (2009a). Die Bewertung von Erwerbseinkommen – Methodische und inhaltliche Analysen zu einer Vignettenstudie im Rahmen des SOEP-Pretest 2008. SOEP papers on Multidisciplinary Panel Data Research, Berlin.

Sauer, C., S. Liebig, K. Auspurg, T. Hinz, A. Donaubauer, J. Schupp (2009b). A Factorial Survey on the Justice of Earnings within the SOEP-Pretest 2008. IZA Discussion Paper No. 4663.

Sauer, C., T. Hinz, K. Auspurg, S. Liebig (2011). The Application of Factorial Surveys in General Population Samples: The Effects of Respondent Age and Education on Response Times and Response Consistency. Survey Research Methods, Vol. 5, No. 3, 89-102.

Sauer, C., P. Valet (2013). Less is Sometimes More: Consequences of Overpayment on Job satisfaction and Absenteeism. Social Justice Research, Published online 14 May 2013, DOI 10.1007/s11211-013-0182-2.

Schelling, T. (1978). Micromotives and Macrobehavior. NY: W. W. Northon & Company.

Scher, S. J. (1997). Measuring the Consequences of Injustice. Personality and Social Psychology Bulletin, Vol 23, No. 5, 482-497.

Schneider F (2002) Size and measurement of the informal economy in 110 countries around the world. Paper presented at the Workshop of Australian National Tax Centre, ANU, Canberra, Australia (http://rru.worldbank.org/Documents/ PapersLinks/informal_economy.pdf), retrieved on 16.05.2013.

Shepelak, N. J., Alwin D. F. (1986). Beliefs about Inequality and Perceptions of Distributive Justice. American Sociological Review, Vol. 51, 30-46.

Shulman, S. (2006). Cultural comparisons and their consequences for nationhood in Ukraine. Communist and Post-Communist Studies, Vol. 39, No. 2, 247-263.

Simončuk, E. (2010). Klassovoje soznanije: opyt sravnitjelnogo empiričeskogo izučenija (Class Consciousness: the Experience of Comparative Empirical Study). Sociologija: teorija, metody, marketing, No. 4, 56-84.

Sinclair, A. G. (1907). Der Utilitarismus bei Sidgwick und Spencer. Heidelberg: Carl Winter's Universitätsbuchhandlung.

Soofi, E.S., J.J. Retzer, M. Yasai-Ardekani (2000). A Framework for Measuring the Importance of Variables with Applications to Management Research and Decision Models. Decision Sciences, Vol. 31, No. 3, 1-31.

Soroka Ju., Zub T. (2008). "Vidmova vid bahatstva" ta zminy u spryjnjatti social'noji nerivnosti. ("Refusal of wealth" and changes in perception of social inequality) Sociolohija: teorija, metody, marketynh, No. 1, 222-236.

Sørensen, A. B. (1998). Theoretical Mechanisms and the Empirical Study of Social Processes. In: P. Hedström, R. Swedberg (eds.), Social Mechanisms: An Analytical Approach to Social Theory, Cambridge: Cambridge University Press, 238-266.

Spell, Ch. S., T. J. Arnold (2007). A Multi-Level Analysis of Organizational Justice Climate, Structure, and Employee Mental Health. Journal of Management. Vol 33, No. 5, 724-751.

Stan korupciji v Ukrajini (2007). Survey report of MSI and KIIS. (http://udscn.guds.gov.ua/files/Dosl/2.pdf), retrieved on 16.05.2013.

Statistisches Bundesamt (2009). Verdienste und Arbeitskosten. Verdienst-strukturerhebung 2006 – Verdienste nach Berufen. Wiesbaden: Statistisches Bundesamt.

Stephenson, S., L. Khakhulina (2000). Russia: Changing Perceptions of Social Justice. In: Mason D. S., J. L. Kluegel (eds.). Marketing Democracy. Lanham: Rowman & Littlefield, 77-97.

Thurstone, L. L. (1928). Attitudes can be measured. American Journal of Sociology, Vol. 33, No. 4, 529-554.

Ukraine: Poverty Update (2007). Report No. 39887 – UA. World Bank. (http://siteresources.worldbank.org/INTUKRAINE/Resources/poverty_update_200707_eng.pdf), retrieved on 16.05.2013.

UNDP (2011). National Human Development Report 2011. Ukraine: Towards Social Inclusion. (http://www.undp.org.ua/files/en_95644NHDR_2011_eng.pdf), retrieved on 16.05.2013.

Vlasenko, N. (2008). Rural Poverty in Ukraine. Problems of Economic Transition. Vol. 51, No. 7, 21-28.

Vorona, V., M. Šulha (eds.) (2010). Ukrajins'ke suspil'stvo 1992-2010. Sociolohičnyj monitorynh. (Ukrainian society 1992-2010. Sociological monitoring). Kyiv: IS NASU.

Vseukrajins'kyj perepys naselennja (2001). (Ukrainian census 2001), (http://www.ukrcensus.gov.ua/), retrieved on 16.05.2013.

Wallace, C., R. Latcheva (2006). Economic Transformation Outside the Law: Corruption, Trust in Public Institutions and the Informal Economy in Transition Countries of Central and Eastern Europe. Europe-Asia Studies, Vol. 58, No. 1, 81-102.

Wallander, L. (2009). 25 Years of Factorial Survey in Sociology: A Review. Social Science Research, Vol. 38, No. 3, 505-520.

Walster, E., G. W. Walster , E. Berscheid (1978). Equity: Theory and Research. Boston: Allyn & Bacon.

Walster, E., G. W. Walster (1975). Equity and Social Justice. Journal of Social Issues, Vol. 31, No. 3, 21-43.

Walzer, M. (1983). Spheres of Justice: a Defence of Pluralism and Equality. New York: Basic Books.

Wegener, B., S. Liebig (1995). Hierarchical and Social Closure Conceptions of Distributive Social Justice: A Comparison of East and West Germany. In: J. R. Kluegel, D. S. Mason, B. Wegener (eds.). Social Justice and Political Change: Public Opinion in Capitalist and Post-Communist States. New York: Walter de Gruyter, 263-284.

Wegener, B., S. Liebig (2000). Is the "Inner Wall" Here to Stay? Justice Ideologies in Unified Germany. Social Justice Research, Vol. 13, No. 2, 177-197.

Wegener, B., B. Lippl, B. Christoph (2000). Justice ideologies, Perceptions of Reward Justice, and Transformation: East and West Germany in Comparison. In: J. R. Kluegel, D. S. Mason (eds.). Marketing Democracy. Changing Opinion about Inequality and Politics in East Central Europe, 122-160.

Wegener, B., S. Steinmann (1995). Justice Psychophysics in the Real World: Comparing Income Justice and Income Satisfaction in East and West Germany. In: Kluegel, J. R., D. S. Mason, B. Wegener (eds.). Social Justice and Political Change. Public Opinion in Capitalist and Post-Communist States. New York: Walter de Gruyter, 151-175.

Welsh, H., J. Kühling, (2013). Income Comparison, Income Formation, and Subjective Well-Being: New Evidence on Envy versus Signaling. SOEP Paper 552.

World Bank (2005). Ukraine: Poverty Assessment, Poverty and Inequality in a Growing Economy. Report No. 34631-UA.

WVS 2006. World Values Survey. Wave 5, 2005-2008 Official aggregate v.20140429. World Values Survey Association (www.worldvaluessurvey.org). Aggregate File Producer: Asep/JDS, Madrid SPAIN.

—. 2011. World Values Survey. Wave 6, 2010-2014 Official aggregate v.20140429. World Values Survey Association (www.worldvaluessurvey.org). Aggregate File Producer: Asep/JDS, Madrid SPAIN.

Yakubovich, V. (2005). Weak Ties, Information, and Influence: How Workers Find Jobs in a Local Russian Labor Market. American Sociological Review. Vol. 70, No. 3, 408-421.

Young, J. T. N., F. Weerman (2013). Delinquency as a Consequence of Misperception: Overestimation of Friends' Delinquent Behavior and Mechanisms of Social Influence. Social Problems, forthcoming.

Zakon Ukrajiny "Pro pensijne zabezpečennja" vid 05.11.1991 (Pension Provision Law of Ukraine) (http://zakon.rada.gov.ua/cgi-bin/laws/main.cgi?nreg=1788-12), retrieved on 16.05.2013.

Zimmerman, W. (1998). Is Ukraine a Political Community? Communist and Post-Communist Studies. Vol. 31, No. 1, 43-55.

Zon, H. van (2001). Neo-Patrimonialism as an Impediment to Economic Development: The Case of Ukraine. Journal of Communist Studies and Transition Politics, Vol. 17, No. 3, 71-95.

INDEX